VISION

On October 14, 1972, Dale and Margi Galloway launched the love-centered ministry of New Hope Community Church. The growth since then has been phenomenal. The membership has caught the vision of their pastor and together they are working toward their goal of 10,000 members in the year 2000.

The New Hope Community Church is located on 14 spectacular acres across the I-205 Freeway from the Clackamas Town Center in southeast Portland, Oregon. The explosion in growth over the last few years has been accelerated by the faithful ministry of Lay Pastors who lead Tender Loving Care Groups each week all over this metropolitan area.

NEW HOPE COMMUNITY CHURCH
11731 S.E. STEVENS RD.
PORTLAND, OREGON 97266
1-503-659-LOVE

VISION

HOW TO CREATE A
SUCCESSFUL CHURCH

DALE E. GALLOWAY

Bible quotations are from the following versions: *The Living Bible* (LB) ©1971 by Tyndale House Publishers, Wheaton, Ill.; *the New International Version* (NIV) ©1978 by the International Bible Society, New York; the *New American Standard Bible* (NAS) ©1977 by The Lockman Foundation, La Habra, Calif.; and the *King James* (KJ).

BOOKS IN PRINT BY AUTHOR
Rebuild Your Life, Scott Publishing
Dare To Discipline Yourself, Revell
12 Ways To A Positive Attitude, Tyndale House
The Fine Art Of Getting Along With Others, Scott Publishing
19 Prime-Time Principles for Success, Scott Publishing
The Awesome Power of Your Attitude, Scott Publishing

Edited by Stanley C. Baldwin
and Don Sheets Jr.

Printed in the United States of America

Published by:
Scott Publishing/ 20/20 Vision, Inc.
PO Box 407
West Linn, OR 97068
1-800-420-2048
ISBN: 1-885605-00-5

Thirteenth Printing, 1996
Revised, Fall 1993

CONTENTS

INTRODUCTION

THEY SAID IT COULDN'T BE DONE

You can't start a denominational church, where they have failed three times before!

With Christ's help I did it.

You can't have small fellowship groups in an old traditional church.

With Christ's help I did it.

You can't start a non-denominational church without any people and without any financial backing in a drive-in theater in rainy Portland, Oregon, and be successful.

With Christ's help I did it.

You cannot break through the barrier of 100 members, 200 members, 500 members, 1000 members, 3000 members, 10,000 members, 25,000 members in America.

**With Christ's help I did it
and with Christ's help I'm going to do it.**

You can't build a Tender Loving Care network with thousands of people meeting every week led by trained, equipped, supervised lay people.

We're doing it.

It was Charles Duell, Director of the United States Patent Office, in 1898, who said, "Everything that can be invented, has been invented." What a foolish, limiting concept this man who was in the position of director of the United States Patent Office had. If people had believed him, the world would have stopped right there.

"20/20 VISION" is written for pastors and church leaders who do not want to stop. They want to charge ahead in building God's church on this earth. I believe in the local church and I have written this book for all who have a desire to see their local church experience growth.

Church growth has been a burning desire of my heart for as long as I can remember. Many of the things that I will share with you I have learned in the school of hard knocks over the past twenty-five years. I'm indebted to men like my father, Dr. Harvey S. Galloway, who was church administrator for thirty years. To Dr. Robert Schuller who has been a source of inspiration and motivation and personal friend to me for the past fourteen years as I have pursued the big dream. To Dr. Paul Cho whose vision and ministry has challenged me to expand my horizons beyond I ever thought possible.

I dedicate this book to my companion and help-mate in creating New Hope Community Church, my wife, Margi Galloway, and to my distinguished staff, friends and pastors, and to the more than 525 lay pastors who work so closely with us in the team ministry of New Hope Community Church.

With this book goes my prayer that as you read it your vision will be enlarged, you will be challenged to go for it in a greater way than you've ever done before. It is true, you do have a **rendezvous with destiny**.

Dale E. Galloway

BREAKING OUT OF THE BOX

No more business as usual! People need the Lord! God wants to use your life to do extraordinary things.

I've had the privilege of knowing super-successful people. What I have discovered is that great people are not that different from you and me. They simply have dreamed bigger dreams, made the decision to go for it and daily walked with God's guidance in taking the steps to success. Great people are ordinary people who become possessed with a cause greater than they are:"For it is God working in you, giving you the will and power to achieve His purposes" (Philippians. 2:13). It is God's will and purpose that your church should be a growing church and that you, personally, along with fellow Christians, should learn how to cooperate with the Holy Spirit in making this a reality.

CHURCHES ARE SUPPOSED TO GROW

Why did Jesus come? If you have read the Bible very much, you know the answer. "He came to seek and save the lost" (Luke 19:10). He was not without a mission. His was the loftiest of missions. What He did was not accidental or temporary. He set in motion a work of God that would be carried on through His church and that would march triumphantly into eternity.

If you want to know God's intention and model for His church, read the Book of Acts. Those first church members were ordinary people but what they did in turning the world upside down for God in cooperation with the Holy Spirit was extraordinary. Their lips were set aflame with the good news of Jesus. Through their lives, God not only added to the church, not only multiplied the church, but created an explosion of church growth on the exponential curve. How did they do it? That's what we are going to rediscover in this book.

How do you flow with the Spirit so that you can be a part of a dynamic church that is exploding in church growth on the exponential curve?

Don't you long to have God use your life in the same way He did those first disciples? Jesus said that we are to make our lives count by doing "greater works than these" (John 14:12). Yes, the work that we are to do in our lifetime for the cause of Christ is to be even greater than the work that Jesus did when He was here on earth. How is this possible? We'll answer that question in the coming pages.

It is disturbing the numbers of good pastors who have been leaving the pastoral ministry for secular employment. Recently a pastor of thirty years of service came to me for help in church growth. With a breaking heart he said, "I am tired of pastoring a dead church. Week after week and nothing of any value happens. We go through the motions. We are just kidding ourselves, we're not doing anything to reach the world for Christ." Then he added, "If it cannot be any different then I'm going to quit the pastoral ministry and go get a secular job."

I understood where my friend was coming from. I, too, pastored a dead church at one time. It just about choked the very life out of me. In the pages ahead I am going to share with you how you can bring new life to a dead church.

My special friend, Harry Vawter, was a great visionary although he spent most of his adult life as a layman ministering in a little dinky church. You know the kind. A new pastor comes and goes every two or three years. No one expects much to happen and nothing does. At times, my friend, Harry, would get himself into some tight spots because his vision was beyond that of the leadership. But his love for Christ and his faithfulness to the church would keep him hanging in there in spite of some misunderstanding and abuse. Harry reminded me of the disciple Andrew; although he was by nature a quiet, shy person, he was a lover of people. He was continually finding some person in need and bringing that person to Jesus.

It was a great thing for me and for Harry when he and his family came to be a part of New Hope Community Church. For the first time his vision for a church that was really reaching unchurched people was fulfilled. In the last years of his life he found rich fulfillment in meaningful service as one of our Lay Pastors. What is a Lay Pastor? I will tell you about this exciting ministry in our church that is open to everyone who wants to do something great for God. The Lay Pastor recruiting, training, motivation, organization, and supervision will all be shared in Part III - PLAN FOR CHURCH GROWTH.

I had the privilege last week of having lunch with a pastor in his early thirties whose small church is in the same area as mine. It thrilled my heart to hear that his vision is to see his church double every year. He came to talk to me because he wanted to glean principles that would make his church a dynamic, growing, exploding church. In Part II - PRINCIPLES FOR CHURCH GROWTH, I will share with you key growth principles that will make any church explode on the exponential curve.

I believe that this is a longing within all of our hearts -- to be in a church that is growing. Church growth is not just for Seoul, Korea, or for Southern California, or for the revival sweeping the third world. It is for every church where pastor and people will pay the price and cooperate with the Holy Spirit to make it happen.

WHY DON'T CHURCHES GROW?

If churches are supposed to grow, then why don't they? New Hope Community Church which my wife, Margi and I launched on October 14, 1972, in Portland, Oregon, the most unchurched city in America, has grown from zero to over 6,000 people. As I write this we are increasing by 1,000 members a year. Some 5,500 people a week attend our more than 500 Tender Loving Care groups, each led by one of our 525 Lay Pastors. But why is this kind of growth the exception instead of the rule?

Why is it that 90% of all churches have less than 300 members? Why is it that 70% of all churches have less than 100 members? These statistics would not be so alarming if it were not for the fact that the majority of these are not new churches, they are churches that have been doing business as usual for years. I first became concerned about the lack of church growth in my early teens, more than 30 years ago. My father, whom I honored and loved, was administrator over 140 churches in Central Ohio. While growing up, I saw and experienced many different kinds of churches. I recall that quarterly my dad would receive reports from each of his pastors. I could not comprehend or understand why quarter after quarter, year after year, the vast majority of these churches would show no growth in membership. Something inside of me said, "This is not right, it is God's will for churches to grow. So what is wrong?"

Upon graduating from seminary in 1963 and entering the pastoral ministry, I made the amazing discovery that church growth was a whole lot easier to talk about than it was to produce. But now, having started two churches which enjoyed phenomenal growth and having pastored two traditional churches where I struggled to bring new life, I am ready to share insights with you which I believe can be used to make any church a growing church.

Why is it that in our times when multitudes are perishing for want of God's love, 90% of the churches are experiencing little or no growth? I believe it is because churches have boxed themselves in. As I have analyzed and prayed about this matter the Lord has brought to my mind twelve boxes that keep churches confined. Through intercessory prayer and the power of the Holy Spirit, churches can break out of these boxes.

TWELVE BOXES THAT STAGNATE THE CHURCH AND STOP THE POWERFUL FLOW OF WHAT GOD WANTS TO DO

BOX 1 - BLINDNESS - In the metropolitan area of Portland, Oregon, where I pastor, more than one million people live. Less than 10% of these have any active membership in a local church. This makes Portland one of the most unchurched cities in America. The need here is overwhelming.

A Christian repairman named Bob was working in the home of one of our members. In the course of their conversation, the two Christians started talking about their respective churches. Our member, very excited about his church, said he participated in a church of thousands of people with many marvelous need-meeting ministries that God was using to give the increase. Bob, not beginning to comprehend what our member was sharing, expressed his narrow viewpoint that he was glad to be in a "little country church" where each person knew the other.

My friend asked Bob where this little country church was located. His answer was unbelievable. That little church is located on a main street in the center of one of the most heavily populated, growing areas of our city. Within 15 minutes of that "little country church" more than 100,000 people live. Ninety thousand of them do not belong to any church.

People never grow or go beyond their vision. No church will ever be any larger than its vision. Tell me your vision and I will tell you your future. If the vision of a church is to be a little country church in the middle of hundreds of thousands of people, that's exactly what that church will be. On the other hand, if a church's vision is to be a growing church then, even though it may be located in a small community, it will be a church that doesn't just survive but thrives. As someone has said, "You will become as small as your controlling desire; as great as your dominant aspiration." The first step to church growth is vision. In Chapter I of this book we will talk about the transcending power of a clear-cut vision.

A couple of summers ago I was at the National Convention of the Christian Booksellers Association held in Anaheim, California, at the Convention Center. I was walking around viewing various publishers' exhibits and visiting with different friends that I met along the way. At a denominational exhibit I met an old friend I hadn't seen in 20 years. In the course of our conversation he asked me about the size of the church that I was pastoring. With some pride and enthusiasm I told him how fast our church was multiplying and that we had a church of thousands of people. His immediate response was, "I don't think a church should be over 200.

I don't want to fault my friend; he was simply reflecting a limiting concept that has plagued that particular denomination for over the last 30 years or more. If you think a church shouldn't be over 200, you can be sure of one thing: Your churches will not be over 200. I think it's time we take the blinders off. It's time to see beyond and break out of the box.

BOX 2 - UNBELIEF - Jesus, the Son of God, the Miracle Worker, could do no miracles in his hometown. Why? Have you ever thought about this? The Scriptures tell us that it was because of their belief. Unbelief stops the mighty works of God.

"Signs and wonders" were nothing extraordinary in the Book of Acts; they were a daily occurrence. Jesus Christ is not dead. He is alive. And He is the same yesterday, today and forever. Just as He worked miracles back then, He works even greater miracles today through the power of the One who lives within us, the Holy Spirit. Yes, with the Holy Spirit we can fulfill the promise of Jesus to do "greater works than these" (John 14:12). In Part I we are going to get into: "POWER FOR CHURCH GROWTH."

My confession is that it has taken me, personally, almost twenty years since finishing seminary to move from operating out of reason and my own resources into the spiritual world of faith and cooperation with the Holy Spirit to do the work of ministry in the church. Since this change has been happening in my life, church growth has been taking place beyond even my fondest boyhood dreams.

Every time we come together at New Hope Community Church, salvation flows, miracles take place, people are renewed in mind and spirit, relations are mended. It seems no matter what I preach on, when it has the anointing of God's Spirit and I flow with His Spirit, people are brought to Christ and their lives are transformed from the inside out.

You, too, can learn to cooperate with the Holy Spirit for "signs and wonders" in your church. But first you must break out of the box of unbelief and learn to win the battle in Jesus' name in the spiritual world. "Jesus said, 'Everything is possible for him who believes'" (Mark 9:23, NIV).

BOX 3 - LACK OF LEADERSHIP - We used to serve communion by having people march around the front in an orderly way to receive the elements and return full circle to their seats. For the serving to work right it depended upon each person following the person in front of him or her. The key to success was to get the first person started correctly.

One Sunday, as people marched around to receive the elements, one person on the end of a row evidently had to go to the rest-room so he went to the back and out the door. An entire row of worshipers followed the wrong leader out the back door. Can you imagine their surprise when they discovered, instead of being led to the communion table, they had been led to the restroom?

This is a good example of what happens when there is no dynamic leader.

When there is not a strong leader, a vacuum is created and anything but good moves into that vacuum.

So much of the confusion in churches today is due to the vacuum that is created because there is not a God-led man or woman who leads the people.

As you study both the Bible and church history, it becomes clear that when great things happened it was always when a man or woman was used of God to lead His people to where He wanted them to go. Sheep cannot lead to anything but confusion. Needed are shepherds who will be leaders.

In Part II, Chapter 1, I will share with you DYNAMIC LEADERSHIP PRINCIPLES.

BOX 4 - SUPERSTAR PASTORS - In this age of electronics, high action entertainment and television, no American church will attract very many people without some "showmanship". People are not going to listen to a preacher no matter how well he knows the Bible unless he becomes a skilled and effective communicator. Before people hear, you must first get their attention. This is why great preparation must go into both the preaching and the music in order for the Celebration Service to attract people.

But in this show-me, entertain-me climate something is happening that harms both the pastors and the people. It is so subtle! It is one of Satan's slyest, most deceitful ways of boxing the church into little or no growth. What am I talking about? I am talking about making pastors professional stars and the people spectators. Everyone has his own ego with its needs. It is so easy for a pastor's ego needs to lead him down the futile path of becoming the congregation's superstar. The same pitfall can trip up other church leaders on a multiple staff.

Where pastors allows themselves to be put in the role of superstar, churches keep going through pastors like a car goes through tires. Why? Because the pastor has allowed himself to be placed in a role with impossible expectations. And, when he does not fulfill the whims and wishes of the spectators then the hero quickly becomes a heel. How many churches do you know where the pastor is a hero for the first two years and then he hits the skids? From then on until he leaves, he is the heel. The truth is, unhappy people need someone to vent their frustrations against.

Participation is the key to success. Lay People who are simply given the role of spectators do not use their spiritual gifts and cannot feel fulfilled. There is nothing that builds one's self-esteem any more than the reality that God is using one's life. And there is nothing that puts purpose into daily living like knowing that what one is doing is a part of God's plan for reaching this world.

God wants to use every person to minister in His name, whether that person is professional clergy or works a secular job. The time has come for churches to break out of the performer box and release lay people into ministry. Throughout this book I will tell you how to do this.

Church growth studies have given us this valuable insight: No matter how good the preaching is, or the teaching, or the music in a particular church, unless people are brought into some kind of small fellowship group they will leave a local church within two or three years and then move on to the next place.

BOX 5 - FOCUS ON DOCTRINE - A salesman friend recently said to me, "Pastor, anyone knows that you don't sell automobiles by talking about the size of the pistons." This was in the context of our conversation about a particular church that we both knew was doctrinally proper and correct but dying. The few people who still went there were being bored to death.

People in our world who are perishing from a variety of diseases of mind, body and soul—which are all the results of being apart from God's love—do not give two hoots about cold doctrine. Do not get me wrong, it's important to have sound doctrine but at New Hope we do not go around showing our bone structure off to hurting people. Our calling is first to heal hurts and build dreams and at the right time and the right place we will instruct people in basic doctrines of the church.

BOX 6 - RUTS - Tradition in the church that I was brought up in dictated every local church hold two revival meetings a year. That was the unwritten law. Any pastor stepping out of that tradition would become suspect of being liberal.

Having never seen any other evangelism method, I mistakenly believed that the only time a person could be saved was at the end of a salvation sermon with the congregation standing and singing an invitation hymn such as "Just As I Am". In my first pastorate, longing to reach unchurched people, I started looking for other methods of evangelism. A whole new world opened up to me when I was led by God into becoming a personal soul winner. Because I broke out of the rut, going to where people were and leading them to Christ, the new church I started in Grove City, Ohio, became a pacesetter of the Central Ohio District, with a growth of 25 new members per year. It stood out among the herd of churches in that denomination.

Today, because I have learned many more ways of reaching people, the church that I pastor sees more people brought to Christ in one week than we did in my first church in an entire year. I am excited to share with you in the coming pages these secrets of exploding evangelism.

My friend, Dr. Robert Schuller, says, "It takes guts to get out of the ruts." Churches are bogged down in the mire of doing what they do simply because they've always done it that way. How important it is to stop and ask these questions: Is this program or activity accomplishing what it was created to accomplish? Is it effective or isn't it effective?

A young couple got married and on their first Sunday together the wife baked a ham. The bridegroom's curiosity was aroused when he saw his wife cut the end off the ham before putting it into the oven. He asked, "Honey, why did you cut the end off the ham?"

She replied, "My mother always did."

Next time the family was together the new husband asked his mother-in-law, "Why do you cut the end off the ham before you bake it?"

Her answer was, "Because my mother always did." Having never really thought about why before, she turned to her mother, "Mother, why did you always cut the end off the ham?"

The grandmother laughed and said, "Oh, honey, because my oven wasn't very big, I had to cut the end off to get it in." It's time we take the lid off the box and stop limiting the work of God by meaningless traditions.

That's not to say that every tradition of ministry is useless. One pastor came to a rather large traditional church and thought it was his calling to do away with every tradition they had. The first thing to go was the Sunday school. Next he did away with the senior citizens ministry. Then he cancelled the July celebration that the church had presented for years. All of these had been good ministry. In a couple of years he left the church worse off than when he came there. All he did was rock the boat and almost sink the ship.

You never do away with anything until you have something better to put in its place. In the pages ahead I am going to share with you many creative, need-meeting ministries that we've established as points of entry to bring people to New Hope Community Church. **In the power of God's Spirit you can then create your own need-meeting ministries which will bring in multitudes of new people.**

BOX 7 - EXCLUSIVE ATTITUDE - One of my friends who is a pastor on our staff told me about a church that did not want any new members. There were only four of them left and out in the cemetery in the church yard only four lots were left. Therefore, they wouldn't dare take in any new members. We laugh at this shortsighted thinking but being exclusive is not a laughing matter. I have in my file a picture taken of a sign that stands in front of a local Methodist Church in the southern part of Oregon. It reads, "Parking for Methodist members only—others will be towed away at owner's expense." Not too inviting I would say.

Some church people are so exclusive, so narrowminded, that their ears touch each other. God's kind of love never excludes— it always reaches out and includes. Someone has said it so well in this little poem:

"He drew a circle that shut me out,
Heretic, rebel, a thing to flout,
But love and I had the wit to win;
We drew a circle that took him in."

At New Hope Community Church, the way we keep reaching out and enlarging the circle is through our Tender Loving Care groups. We have more than 500 Tender Loving Care Groups that reach out to include and bring in others. This is how we keep breaking out of the box to enlarge the circles of love to always include one more.

What is a Tender Loving Care group? In Part III, Chapter 3, I will answer this question in detail so you too can break out of the box, and enlarge your boundaries.

BOX 8 - ISOLATION - I asked a neighboring pastor, "How many visitors do you have at your church each Sunday?" He hung his head and confessed that they went months without having any visitors. How can a church grow without visitors? The answer is obvious.

One of the boxes that is confining so many churches to little or no growth is a social problem. Too many Christians have isolated themselves from non-Christian people. They have nothing to do with them, let alone relating to them in such a way as to bring them to Christ. The majority of people who are brought to a growing church are brought there by a friend. There is no evangelism like friendship evangelism. It is not dependent upon ability or a super program. It just happens in the natural flow of a Christian relating out of love and concern to a non-Christian.

I had a conversation yesterday with one of our new Christians and learned that he had already brought several other new families to New Hope Community Church. With a big smile he told me he was going to bring dozens of other new people. Excited about what Jesus had done in his life he was serving the Lord with enthusiasm.

In a doctor's office at the bottom of a space exploration picture I read these words: "Science is at the moving edge of what's happening." I thought to myself, a church that is really concerned about fulfilling the "great commission" is one that is at the moving edge of what's happening in people's lives. We are to be the Master's hands in love extended. You can't win people unless you get involved in their lives. In the pages ahead I am going to tell you many different ways that your church can live on the edge of what's happening and when it does, it will become a growing church.

BOX 9 - IMPOSSIBILITY THINKING - Impossibility thinking not only warps the mind but it dwarfs churches. Jesus presented Philip with an enormous opportunity. He asked him, *"How do we feed this multitude of 5,000 men, plus children and women?" (John 6:5).* The question He asks of you is much the same. "How are we going to feed all these spiritually hungry, starving people who are all around your church? How do we reach them?"

Philip immediately saw all the reasons why it couldn't be done. He said, *"We don't have enough money. There aren't any stores for miles. Better have a committee meeting to see if we can't come up with more reasons why it can't be done."*

Those who operate out of the negative can immediately spot reasons why church growth can never occur in their church. There are always excuses if that's what you're looking for. The miracle of the feeding of the 5,000 would never have happened if it had depended upon Philip. And the miracle of lives being transformed and changed through the power of God will not happen where people choose to be impossibility thinkers.

Thank God for Andrew who not only saw the opportunity but looked for the possibilities of what he could do to set the miracle in motion. "Some men see things as they are and say,'why?' I dream things that never were and say,'why not?'" (George Bernard Shaw)

Andrew believed that with God nothing was impossible so he started looking for the possibility and he found a little boy with a few Twinkies and sardines. When we believe in the God of the impossible, we start looking for the answer to how God wants to use us to feed the multitude.

I believe that it's possible for your church to break out of the box and to experience glorious growth.

BOX 10 - BUSYNESS I know a pastor who is busy all the time, yet his church shows no growth. In fact the truth is, his church is on a descending scale. What's wrong? The problem is that he and his people are busy doing a whole bunch of things that don't really count. They give no thought to majoring on what's essential instead of diddling their lives away on non-essentials.

Every church needs to have clear-cut objectives and goals in order to keep on target. In the early days of our ministry we hammered out these objectives and purposes for New Hope Community Church:

1. Reach unchurched thousands.
2. Be a healing center
3. Be an edifying center
4. Be an equipping center
5. Build strong Christian families
6. Offer Christ-centered, positive inspiration
7. Be a deploying center
8. Be a worship center

Along with this we have clear-cut goals to keep us on target with our objectives and purposes. In the pages ahead I will help you to discover and work toward the goal of your church with singleness of purpose.

BOX 11 - AIMLESSNESS - Aim at nothing, and you will succeed. As my friend, Dr. Robert Schuller, has said thousands of times, "Fail to plan and you plan to fail." The longer I'm in the ministry, the more I recognize the importance of taking the time for good planning. Nothing happens unless the leaders of a church plan for it to happen. Don't wait for your ship to come in, swim out to it.

I have spent my life planning for church growth. It's not by accident that the church I'm pastoring is exploding on the exponential curve. Growing churches expect to grow in advance. Life is a self-fulfilling prophecy. I will share with you our plan in detail for even greater explosive growth along with giving you some real help in formulating your own plan and putting it into action. This will be happening in Part III - PLAN FOR CHURCH GROWTH. Remember this, "Details determine destiny."

BOX 12 - PRIDE - Whenever I speak at church growth conferences or have a chance to speak with a church leader, I like to ask this question. "What are you doing in your church, in your ministry, that there is no way you can accomplish it without the help and power of God?"

Our worst enemy is pride. This is why the Scripture warns us, *"Pride goeth before a fall."* The Scripture also teaches us, *"God giveth grace to the humble but resisteth the proud and the arrogant" (I Peter 5:5).*

A large number of people on our staff and in our Lay Pastor ministry have been broken. But God is now using them to bless. The reason God can use their lives is that they know who their source is and where their help comes from. As they fellowship with the Holy Spirit, they are living in dependency upon the Lord and so grateful to God that He is using their lives in meaningful ministry.

There's no greater lesson for us to learn than "depend on the Lord." It is my petition for you that as I share my own personal walk with Jesus—and struggles and victories in ministry—that there will be created within you a deep hunger to know God better. And an urgent desire to depend upon the Lord that out of your brokenness will come great blessing.

THERE ARE ONLY TWO KINDS OF CHURCHES

There are only two kinds of churches, and I don't mean Catholic and Protestant. In fact there are many different names that appear over the doors of churches but it's not the name that really distinguishes what kind of church it is. Some churches are formal and some informal, some are denominational churches while others are independent. But all churches are either dead or alive. Is your church dead or is it alive? This book is dedicated to making churches alive.

An internationally known planner, Edmond Bacon, says, "A city becomes great when its people begin aspiring to greatness." What I would like to say to you is this: "A church becomes great when its people begin aspiring to greatness." And greatness in God's sight, I believe, means church growth (See Matthew 28:18-20).

Preceding the launching of New Hope Community Church on October 14, 1972, my darling wife, Margi, and I sat in the Prayer Chapel on the 14th floor of Dr. Schuller's Tower of Hope. We were attending the Institute for successful Church Growth.

In the last message Dr. Schuller said these words, "The greatest churches ever built in America have not even been started yet. Someone here will build a greater church yet, with seven day a week activities! It will be a sensation for Christ." I believe that

New Hope Community Church is on the way to becoming one of these churches that Dr. Schuller prophesied. As I write these words we are already exploding on the exponential curve but believe that we just have the foundations in well.

Last summer in Seoul, Korea, Dr. Paul Cho challenged the church leaders there with his vision, that there would be built in every major city in America a church with 100,000 members.

I believe God has given His vision to Dr. Cho and that vision will become others' clear-cut vision. In the pages ahead I will detail to you what I believe is God's master plan for creating exploding churches.

PART I
POWER FOR CHURCH GROWTH

PART I - POWER

CHAPTER 1 - POWER OF VISION

Margi and I had the privilege of spending four days together with pastors and their wives from 15 of the super churches of America. The setting was Dr. Robert Schuller's fabulous retreat center at Rancho Capistrano in Southern California. To be invited to this creative retreat, one had to be the senior pastor of a church that had a Sunday attendance of more than 2500 people. Responding to the invitation to come and meet with Dr. Schuller for four days were senior pastors from Presbyterian, Methodist, Southern Baptist, Assemblies of God, Lutheran and Reformed churches, and pastors from several independent congregations.

We spent four days together sharing in Christian love and ministry. I was struck by the uniqueness of each leader's personality. Besides having a deep love for God and people, these very different leaders had one thing in common. Do you know what it was? **They were all persons of visions and dreams**.

In this first chapter I want to share with you about the "Transcending Power of a Vision."

Several years ago I was in Columbus, Ohio, on a Sunday morning. Columbus, the home of the Ohio State Buckeyes, is where I was brought up. That morning I got up early, had breakfast, and then drove out southwest to the suburb of Grove City, where I attended the Sunday morning service at the Nazarene Church.

Of all the churches in Columbus, why did I choose to attend this service? Because twenty years before, in 1963, upon my graduation from seminary I accepted the vision to create a new Church of the Nazarene in Grove City, Ohio. To go there and begin a new church was fulfillment of a vision and dream that I had conceived at fifteen years of age and carried with me through college and seminary.

As I launched this new work, my clear-cut vision was of a church that would someday have 400 members and be the largest Nazarene Church in Central Ohio. When I left there four years later, the church had approximately 100 members and was a pacesetter in growth in the denomination. While there I had led the church in purchasing three acres in the center of the city, built the first building and then added an educational wing, and planted in their hearts and minds the vision of the final sanctuary that would seat approximately 400 people.

Now here I was, sixteen years after having left as pastor, sitting in the third row from the front, in the exact sanctuary I had envisioned years before. I counted the number of people present. Do you know how many people were present that Sunday morning? There were 400 people.

All of a sudden this realization hit me like a ton of bricks. This local church, after twenty years, was the exact size of my vision that I had for it before it ever was. No smaller and no bigger.

That day Jesus spoke to my heart through His Spirit and said, *"According to your faith so be it."*

Before launching New Hope Community Church in Portland, Oregon on October 14, 1972 I had a clear-cut vision that the church would be a church for the unchurched thousands. My vision was that we would have 1000 members at the end of ten years. The size of my vision was limited by the framework of the denomination in which I was reared. When I was a boy growing up in a church administrator's home, the largest church our denomination had was one with 1000 members. So that became my ceiling for how large I thought a church could become. After nine-and-one half years we reached the goal of having our first 1000 members. Having broken through that barrier, it took less than two years to get the second thousand members. And now, the third thousand members have come in less time than that. The bigger the vision, the bigger the church is going to become. The most miraculous things happen when someone gets a clear-cut vision.

WHAT IS A VISION?

A vision is the ability, or the God-given gift, to see those things which are not as becoming a reality. A vision is described in the Word of God in Hebrews 11:1 in this definition of faith: *"Now faith is the substance of things hoped for, the evidence of things not seen."* To paraphrase: "Faith is vision and vision is seeing it long before it is."

HOW IMPORTANT IS A VISION?

I heard a story about a gang of laborers digging a hole five feet square by ten feet deep. After grueling hours of hard labor, they finally got the hole dug. The boss had never bothered to tell them the purpose for digging the hole. In fact, after they got the hole all dug, he looked at them and said, "Fill it back up."

Immediately the men walked off the job and said, "We quit, we want our pay now!"

When the boss asked why, they replied, "Digging holes and filling them up only makes fools of us."

Then the boss took the time to explain to them the purpose for digging the hole. It was to locate a leaking gas line that was endangering the health of the people who lived in that area. Once they found out there was purpose in their digging they became satisfied and remained on the job.

Deep down within everyone of us is a need to make our lives count. There is nothing like an all-consuming vision to give to our lives the meaning and purpose we long for.

Without a vision, life is humdrum and routine. The Bible says, *"Without a vision the people perish (Proverbs 29:18)*. How true! But with a vision, life becomes exciting; every day is a new adventure.

With a vision people not only tackle the impossible but accomplish it. Without a vision, little worthwhile is ever attempted. Good things do not happen by accident.

A CHURCH WITHOUT A VISION IS A BORING CHURCH

A fellow told me that he was visiting a church on his vacation. During the morning service the pastor called all the board members to the platform. One fellow went up who obviously was not a member of the board. The pastor at first looked perplexed and then, right in front of everyone, asked the man, "Are you sure you are on the board?"

The man said, "Say, pastor, if anyone here is more bored than I am, I'd like to meet him."

How important is a vision? People without a vision can't even survive let alone thrive. It is a vision that adds excitement and enthusiasm to the life of people. My heart aches for the scores of churches where it's just boring business as usual. Yesterday I was having lunch with a new staff member. With tears in his eyes he told me how badly he felt for some of his friends who have little or no joy in their Christian life because for years they have been members of a church without vision. Yes, they love Jesus but they attend church and serve not with enthusiasm but out of duty.

WHERE DO VISIONS AND DREAMS COME FROM?

God wants to work through the function of our minds called VISUALIZATION to accomplish His work on this earth. Great blessings come to us first by seeing. Consider how God worked with Abraham. *"And he brought him forth abroad, and said, 'Look now toward heaven, and tell the stars, if thou be able to number them:' and he said unto him, 'So shall thy seed be'"* *(Genesis 15:5)*.

God told Abraham to look up to the sky and count the stars but those stars became countless and God said, *"Abraham, your seed, your descendants, will be as numerous as those stars."*

In that moment Abraham's eyes were filled with joyful tears as he saw himself becoming the father of a great nation.

You need to understand that up until this time Abraham and his wife, Sarah, had been barren. They had been unable to have a child and were now well past the age of child bearing. In fact, when Sarah first heard of Abraham's vision she laughed out loud. It was ridiculous, impossible. Abraham must be crazy.

It's not unusual for men and women who have God's vision to be thought crazy. Wait until you hear the vision that God has given the writer of this book.

The thing that we must see is that the mighty miracle—God giving to Abraham his son, Isaac, and making him father of the nation of Israel—began with Abraham's vision. The vision became the creative instrument through which God did His mighty work.

The truth that I am seeing clearly is that being used, mightily used, of God begins with getting God's vision for your life.

THE HOLY SPIRIT IS THE TRANSPORTER
OF VISIONS AND DREAMS

In Acts 2:17 we learn that when the Holy Spirit comes upon us He will give us visions and dreams. *"And it shall come to pass in the last days, saith God, I will pour out of my Spirit upon all flesh: and your sons and your daughters shall prophesy, and your young men shall see visions, and your old men shall dream dreams."*

As we learn to fellowship with the Holy Spirit, He acts as God's messenger planting in our minds and hearts the seed thoughts of dreams and visions. I want to tell you that when you live in the land of visions and dreams with God, life is changed from ordinary to extraordinary. A day isn't just a day, it becomes a special day.

Men and women of vision and dreams have no trouble praying because they have something to pray about.

Men and women of vision and dreams have no trouble tithing because they believe in it wholeheartedly.

Men and women of vision and dreams have no trouble believing God for big things because they know that God can do the impossible.

Men and women of vision and dreams have no trouble with drifting and laziness because they know where they're going and they're turned on for Jesus.

Men and women of vision and dreams find themselves setting measurable, realistic, motivating, and attainable goals though not easy goals that don't challenge faith.

Our calling from God is to learn the life of the Spirit and to be men and women of visions and dreams.

HOW LARGE CAN A CHURCH BECOME?

At the retreat for senior pastors from super churches, I asked how large a church can become. No one had an answer. The Scriptures tell us, *"Nothing is impossible with God."* The tragic thing is that most church leaders are more interested in how big a church CAN'T become than they are in how big it can become.

What's needed in today's society is men and women of vision who will see the church not as a little country church but as the great supermarket meeting the complexity of needs that people have in our society today. It takes a big church to have the need-meeting ministries that will adequately serve people today. The larger the church, the more ministries it can have to meet people at their need. The stronger a church becomes, the greater its impact will be in the community. The bigger the church, the bigger the net. And as you know, the bigger the net, the more fish you are going to catch.

THE EXPONENTIAL CURVE

A majority of churches have little or no growth. Some have a slow addition. A few have multiplication. My prayer is for a score of churches that will get on the exponential curve. The exponential curve is like a snowball going down the mountain. As it goes, it picks up momentum until you have multiplication times multiplication times multiplication which equals explosion.

At our local church we are at the beginning of the exponential curve. In our twelve years of history we have had more than 28% increase per year. For the last three years we have been growing in excess of 500 new members per year. My vision is that this rate will continue and the number of new members per year will accelerate.

IT ALL BEGINS WITH A VISION

Tell me your vision and I will tell you your future. What is your vision for your church? How many members do you expect to have in five years, ten years, twenty years from now?

Before you can receive the vision that God has placed in your mind you must take the limits off your mind.

Let me tell you about a little experience I had while visiting Dr. Cho's church in Seoul, Korea. I went there with other ministers as a part of his World Conference on International Growth. They put us up at the first class Lotte Hotel in downtown Seoul.

My room was on the 17th floor. The first five days I was there I thought that I was staying near the top of the hotel because the elevator I rode every day had a panel on it that showed it went as high as the 22nd floor. I mean I thought I was right up there at the top.

Then on the sixth morning, just the day before I came home, they told us we were going to have breakfast on the 36th floor. I didn't even imagine there were higher floors, because I had a restricting limitation in my mind.

Many people have self-imposed, built-in limitations on their minds. God can do this but He can't do any more. What I want to do is to take off all the limits. What I want you to do is to take the limits off your mind. Open up to God's big vision. Open up to the beautiful consuming dream.

SEVEN THINGS TO DO TO BRING YOUR VISION TO A REALITY

I - *PICTURE* - GET A CLEAR-CUT PICTURE OF THE VISION IN YOUR MIND

Your mind has within it a capability for picture making that the finest cameras being manufactured do not have. A camera can only take a picture of what is already physically visible; within your creative imagination is the marvelous ability to picture what has not yet happened. When this happens, creativity is released and goes to work.

Bill Glass, the former all-pro football player now turned national evangelist, tells this story. A young woman had given birth to a child prematurely. The baby had to be kept on a support system in the nursery away from the mother. Separated from her child, the mother found her milk would not come in. Then a nurse got the bright idea of making a picture of the new infant with a polaroid camera and then placing the picture where the mother could enjoy seeing her new daughter. As the mother looked at the picture, guess what happened. Her milk came in.

Many years ago, even before I launched the ministry of New Hope Community Church, God gave to me a clear-cut vision as to the kind of property on which we were to build. I shared this vision with our first leaders and it became the fixed vision of the church. We saw that our building, for ministry to thousands of people was to be located on a major freeway, on a lush, beautiful hillside. It was to have visibility and good accessibility. It was to be a breath-taking spot of beauty that would inspire people. This describes exactly where New Hope Community Church is located today, with the added benefit that we are directly across the freeway from one of the largest shopping centers in the State of Oregon. It all began with a clear-cut picture in the mind.

Many of the need-meeting ministries that we have at New Hope Community Church were first pictured in the mind of some individual member. We just completed our 12th annual Family Camp held at the Friends Twin Rocks Camp on the Oregon coast. It was a delightful, fun time for all ages as we celebrated Christian life in the family together. Hundreds of people were present and benefitted from this family camp experience.

How did we ever start having family camps? One of our lay people got a picture in his mind of a camp where all ages of people would enjoy each other. He came to me and shared his vision with me and I accepted it as being a beautiful idea from God. Over the years, that picture has grown into a marvelous camping experience that hundreds of our people benefit from and enjoy. It all started when one of our lay persons got a picture in his mind.

What picture has God placed in your mind? What is the vision in ministry that God has given to you? The first step in seeing something beautiful become a reality is to get a clear-cut picture of the vision in your mind.

II - *HEART* - COMMIT YOURSELF TO THE FULFILLMENT OF THE VISION

Before you're ready to move on fulfilling your vision it must get down into your heart. I remember watching a high school football team with limited talent defeat a championship team of superior skills. The team that had less ability won because on that night they had more heart. They put themselves completely into the game and played beyond their ability. Their burning desire gave them the win.

If you are going to do something great for God you can count on facing obstacles. The greater your vision, the bigger and more frequent the obstacles you're going to face. When the going gets tough, those who do not have their hearts in it give up.

When our youngest child, Scott, was six years of age, he learned to ride his bicycle without training wheels on our summer family vacation. Previously he had been riding his bike only with training wheels. But on this one particular morning my wife, Margi, and I decided it was time the training wheels come off and Scott learn to ride his bike on his own.

At first, Scott was convinced that he couldn't do it so he didn't try very hard. But I got up right beside him while he was trying to ride and kept talking to him. "You can do it, Scott. It's going to be so much fun to ride without training wheels. You can do it! Just pedal faster."

All of a sudden the picture of riding without wheels took hold, got down inside of him where a burning desire began to flame, and before I knew it, he took off riding. I found myself yelling at him, "Slow down, slow down!" as I went running all out of breath trying to catch up with a runaway bicycle rider.

It's not going to happen until you get your heart in it. Jesus said, *"Where your treasure is there will your heart be also (Matthew 6:21).* What you place value on, that is what is going to have your heart. In the Bible the word "heart" means the center of your affections. To fulfill a great vision you've got to want it with all your heart.

The psalmist said it this way, *"Delight thyself also in the Lord; and he will give you the desires of your heart" (Psalm 37:4).* Upon graduation from seminary in the year 1963, which now has been more years than I like to remember, I had a vision that I would become a personal soul winner. This became a burning desire within me. Even though I had been brought up in a church, gone to a Christian college and graduated from one of the finest seminaries in this country, I didn't even know how to lead someone personally to Jesus Christ. But I had a burning desire.

When I got up in the morning I began my day by praying to God that He would make me a soul winner. Various times in the day I would cry out to God that He would help me to lead someone to Him. It was a burning flame within me. The picture of being a soul winner and my desire to be one caused me to read every book I could find on the subject of personal soul winning. This earnest seeking to fulfill the vision went on for days and months.

Then God brought a young man into my life, in answer to my prayer, who in five minutes showed me how to use Scripture to lead someone personally to Jesus Christ. That very afternoon I went visiting in the home of one of the people I was working with and led him to Jesus Christ. I was so excited. Wow! When I left there I went to another house and led that whole family to Christ. That was the beginning of a life of personal soul winning. It never would have happened without a burning desire in my heart. To fulfill your vision you've got to get it down in your heart.

III - *SOUL* - PRAY THROUGH UNTIL YOU KNOW YOUR VISION IS GOD'S WILL FOR YOUR LIFE

Two of the church leaders that Margi and I enjoyed fellowshipping with at the Super Church gathering were Bishop John and Mary Lee Meares, pastor and wife of the Evangel Temple in Washington, D. C. Their church was recently featured as one of the outstanding churches of America in *Charisma* magazine. John and Mary Lee are white and have the privilege and distinction of pastoring an all-black congregation in the center of our National Capital.

Their story is one of the most inspiring that I have ever heard. John is a man of vision and dreams and tremendous compassion.

More than 30 years ago he went to Washington with a vision to build a great church in the center of that city. He had heart and a commitment to that vision.

John began with evangelistic healing crusades. Large numbers of people came but as time passed John clearly saw that there must be a teaching ministry. These people who lived in the inner city needed the gospel in order to make heaven their home. However, they also needed help in becoming what God had created them to be. So John began a ministry of teaching the people how to realize their potential and become everything God had created them to be.

In the early years his congregation was made up of both blacks and whites. It was an integrated congregation. Then in the sixties when riots flared and the city was in a turmoil, the whites, out of fear, fled. John and his wife stayed. One Sunday rioters came into the congregation to attack the white pastor and his wife. The men of John's congregation bodily picked up the rioters and threw them out the front door.

Why did John stay when everyone else left? Because years before he had prayed through and had the assurance in his heart that his vision came from God. Thirty-four years later he has a black congregation of thousands of people. And he has witnessed miracle after miracle as his people have moved from welfare to being successful in business, professions and leadership positions in Washington.

Recently his church purchased a 400-acre parcel of land upon which to further create the vision of ministry that God has placed in their hearts. The way to test a dream is to pray it through until you know that you know this is God's vision and dream for your life.

IV - *FOCUS* - CONCENTRATE ON THE FULFILLMENT OF THE VISION

So many people never achieve in their life because they scatter in all directions. To fulfill a great vision takes singleness of mind. It has been said that what gets your attention gets you. To fulfill a vision you must concentrate on the fulfillment of the vision.

I remember as a boy, owning a magnifying glass. I would go out in the backyard when the sun was shining and focus that magnifying glass on a leaf. As I concentrated the rays of the sun on that leaf, it would burst into flames. One day as I was starting to focus my magnifying glass on a leaf, a dog ran by and I forgot what I was doing and ran after the dog. I lost the concentration and consequently what I had set out to do didn't happen.

If you are going to achieve your dream, it's going to take a lot of concentration. It's going to mean denying lesser things to gain this greater vision.

V - *ORGANIZE* - TO ACCOMPLISH THE VISION

God has a Master Plan for us to enter into explosive church growth. This plan is not a new idea with me but was used in the early church's growth explosion. It is what I call 20/20 vision because it is found in Acts 20:20. *"And how I kept back nothing that was profitable unto you, but have shown you, and have taught you publicly and from house to house." (Also see Acts 5:14 and Acts 5:41).*

In the early church they met together for the giant celebration on the Resurrection Day of the week. And during the week they met from house to house in small cell groups.

The power of the house-to-house plan can be seen in the modern miracle that has occurred in Red China, where today there are an estimated fifty million Christians. How could this be? Few or no church buildings. No public services. For decades, no professional clergy. It's been against the law with the threat of death even to be a practicing Christian.

No one had any idea how many millions of Christians there were in Red China until recently. Apparently, the government had a time in which they invited all the Christians to declare themselves. In the back of their minds they thought they would get Christianity out in the open and then they could wipe it out. But to their utter dismay, so many Christian people stepped forward that the government was helpless to do anything about it. They couldn't exterminate 50,000,000 people.

How did this modern phenomenon happen? It happened because they discovered God's Master Plan for evangelizing the world. They met in homes in small groups. Often they met after midnight in the wee hours of the morning so they would not be detected by the government. They read the Bible together. They prayed for each other through the power of God's Spirit. They shared their faith together. And one by one they brought their friends out of darkness into the light of Jesus.

To accomplish our vision, we presently divide the metropolitan area into four districts, led by four district pastors. They are assisted by assistant pastors in supervising and motivating 525 lay pastors, who lead more than 500 Tender Loving Care groups meeting weekly. Close to 5,500 people meet in these Tender Loving Care groups. We already have in place an organization with no limits to its ability to keep expanding. By keeping up with the growth, we make possible even greater exponential growth. At New Hope Community Church we are freeing and equipping lay people for meaningful ministry. I will share the details of this with you in PART III---PLAN FOR CHURCH GROWTH.

VI - *RISK* - RISK FAILURE TO GAIN SUCCESS OF YOUR VISION

Right after World War II the two giant retailers in America made two very different decisions affecting their separate destinies. One was the Sears Roebuck Company while the other was Montgomery Ward.

The leadership of Ward's expected that after the war would come an economic depression, so they pulled back and refused to take any risk in expanding.

Meanwhile, the leadership of Sears determined that there was going to be economic growth such as America had never seen before. So they went out and expanded into new markets all over the country. As a result, Sears soared ahead while Ward's fell far behind. Sears took the risk, they risked failure and thus gained greater success. Ward's pulled back and today is still suffering the consequences of their unwillingness to take the risk.

I'm not talking about irresponsible, reckless risk, but I am talking about faith-based risk. After doing all the research, after seeking the best counsel possible, there comes a time when you've got to go for it.

Success is a process. If you ever stop going for it, then you stop being successful. Success is like stairsteps, one step builds on the former step while preparing for the next step.

In our ministry at New Hope Community Church we have never gone to a new peak without being willing to risk it all. But I for one, would rather attempt something great for God and fail than do nothing and succeed.

VII - *FAITH* - PUT INTO ACTION YOUR FAITH IN THE VISION THAT GOD HAS GIVEN YOU

Before a vision can become a reality it must begin to be verbalized in spoken words of faith. Visions verbalized in words of faith release the creative powers of God to work through our lives, to bring into existence that which was not.

Early in the beginning days of our ministry of New Hope, God gave me a burden for single people. I envisioned that we would have a great need-meeting ministry in their lives. I shared this consuming vision with my friend and fellow pastor, Rich Kraljev, and it also became his vision. For months we prayed together about the launching of this vision.

On Easter Sunday, 1977, knowing that God's timing was now, we launched the Positive Singles ministry. Without any people we visualized and spoke the words of faith by advertising in the Oregonian the following: "100 Christian Men at New Hope's Positive Singles." Then we gave the time and place. We not only visualized that we would have men but we spoke words of faith based on the assurance in our hearts that this was what God wanted.

Once I began to grasp this spiritual truth in cooperation with the Holy Spirit I started speaking the words of salvation at the conclusion of my message. Now, week after week, no matter what I preach on there is a flow of salvation. Large numbers of people stand, pray the sinner's prayer and commit their lives to Jesus Christ.

This principle is evidenced further with the completion of our 3000-seat auditorioum, which was constructed in less than 12 months. In cooperation with the Holy Spirit, we spoke words of faith and participated in the creation of a marvelous miracle. A vision which has now become a reality at New Hope Community Church!

I want to clarify this point. It's not that you just stand up and say something and it automatically happens. That is not faith in action—that is foolishness. That's just speaking words.

What you need to understand is that there is an incubation period, just as a period of time must pass before a baby is born. Spend time with your vision in fellowship with the Holy Spirit, clarifying, crystallizing that vision. Purify your motives and desires, and make sure that God wants to use your life to make this thing happen. Pray through and get the assurance in your heart that this is God's will for your life. Make sure you find His perfect timing.

Then, like Moses of old to whom God gave the vision to deliver the children of Israel out of Egypt, take the word that God has given to you and stand up and speak the words.

For years Moses prepared and got ready. In Exodus 14 we see that as a result of the ten plagues, the children of Israel are on the march out of bondage when they come to the Red Sea. Suddenly they are frightened. Before them is this impossible huge body of water. Behind them is the heavily armed Egyptian army. They panic and cry out, *"What shall we do?"*

"Then the Lord said to Moses, 'Why are you crying out to me? Tell the Israelites to move on. Raise your staff, stretch your hand over the sea to divide the water so the Israelites can go through the sea on dry land.'"

And when Moses gave the command, spoke the words, God used his words to create a miracle. The sea was parted and the Israelites marched through the open sea to safety on the other side.

I dare you to become pregnant with a vision for growth on the exponential curve in your local church. I am convinced that God wants not only to do great things through our lives *"but greater things than these" (John 14:12)*.

**SEE GREAT THINGS FOR GOD
ATTEMPT GREAT THINGS FOR GOD
AND REALIZE GREAT THINGS FOR GOD**

PART I - POWER

CHAPTER 2 - POWER OF THE HOLY SPIRIT

It is not by accident that Jesus instructed His disciples with these words: *"Do not leave Jerusalem, but wait for the gift my Father promised, which you have heard me speak about. For John baptized with water, but in a few days you will be baptized with the Holy Spirit" (Acts 1:4-5, NIV).* **Jesus knew that without the Holy Spirit the disciples would fall flat on their faces. We are not different from them.** Without the Holy Spirit we are like a balloon without air. Like a car without gas. We can never begin to accomplish our mission successfully in this world if we do not know and cooperate with the Holy Spirit.

It was not by accident that the birth of the church and its launching into ministry in this world occurred simultaneously with the disciples being filled with the Holy Spirit. The church's very life and growth is dependent upon the Holy Spirit. Without the Holy Spirit there is no alive church, only a dead carcass or memory of better days, or regrets of what might have been. The only power that can raise churches from the dead is the Holy Spirit.

It was not by accident that when Jesus said we would do "greater works than these," it was in the context of teaching us about the powerful One who would not only be with us but live in us. How can we do greater works than Jesus did? Through the power of the Holy Spirit (John 14:12).

When Zerubbabel, the governor of Judea, was facing insurmountable difficulties in the construction work on the house of the Lord, Zechariah the prophet, told him, *"'Not by might nor by power, but by my Spirit,' says the Lord Almighty"* *(Zechariah 4:6, NIV)*.

I remember when my fun-loving, inquisitive son, who was then eight years old, came to me with a very serious concern. He said, "Dad, is the Holy Spirit a ghost?" Then, as if he had a second thought on the matter, he continued his questioning with these words, "Or is the Holy Spirit like a cloud floating around?"

Right there I sent up a quick cry for help to my helper, the Holy Spirit, on how to make Him better known to my son, Scott. I said to Scott, "Have you ever felt real close to God?" He nodded his head as if he understood exactly what I was talking about. Then I pointed out to him, "That was the Holy Spirit."

Yes, the Holy Spirit is something more than a ghost. Something more than a cloud. He is a person that you can know personally.

The Holy Spirit is something more than a cold doctrine. There are churches that have lots of doctrine about the Holy Spirit, but unfortunately not much life in the Spirit. This is evidenced by business as usual week after week with little or no annual church growth. The letter of the law kills, while the Spirit of the Lord frees.

The Holy Spirit is something more than the born again experience. Yes, it's true. We are born of the Spirit. It is the Spirit's work that brings us into a relationship with Jesus Christ. It is the Holy Spirit who transforms us and makes us a new person. But the Holy Spirit is something more than the one who causes the new life to happen within us. He IS the life. Yes, the Holy Spirit is something more, so much more.

The Holy Spirit is more than one, two, or three ecstatic experiences. From the Book of Acts and from Christians' personal testimonies of being filled with the Holy Spirit, I concluded that there are different experiences. Some have a very emotional experience while others have a very quiet experience. Some can point to the exact time and the day on the calendar when they were filled with the Holy Spirit. Others have had a progressive release in receiving the Spirit and cannot tell you the exact time. When people were filled with the Holy Spirit, some spoke in tongues while others didn't. My conclusion is that every Christian needs to experience the Holy Spirit personally. But any experience, no matter how genuine or how wonderful, is meant to be not an ending but a beginning, not a monument but a momentum. Yes the Holy Spirit is something more, so much more.

Who is the Holy Spirit? Someone greater than you are.

I cannot be successful as Senior Pastor of New Hope Community Church without a whole lot of help from Someone greater than I am. **The truth is that I cannot even live the Christian life with victory and success without a power greater than I am.**

Far too many drifting Christians are unaware of the fact that we are in a spiritual world where the battle is raging for the souls of men, women and children (See Ephesians 5:10-19).

In the spiritual world there are three spirits: God's Spirit, Satan's spirit, and the human spirit. All three of these spirits have power. Don't ever underestimate the power of the enemy of your soul. And we have to acknowledge that wonderful things happen through the efforts and power of people working together for common achievement. But there is no greater power than God's power. God is the ultimate power. Thank God for this present reality, *"Greater is he that is in you than he that is in the world" (I John 4:4, KJ)*.

1. THE HOLY SPIRIT IS A PERSON

This Greater One is the Holy Spirit. **The Holy Spirit is a person.** God is Father, Son and Holy Spirit. I have found the person of the Holy Spirit to be all of the following and so much more:

Teacher (John 14:26, NAS)
Guide (I Thessalonians 5:19)
Convictor (John 16:8-12)
Comforter (John 16:7)
Cleanser (Acts 15:8)
Interceder (Romans 8:26-27)
Helper (Romans 8:26, NAS)
Miracle worker (Acts 2:4; 8:39)
Commander (Acts 8:29; 13:2; Acts 5)

Gentleman (John 1:32-33)
Enabler (Ephesians 3:16)
Bringer of wisdom (James 1:5)
Creator (Hebrews 11:3)
Motivator (II Timothy 1:7)

In her marvelous book on the Holy Spirit entitled *The Helper*, Catherine Marshall tells a story about a woman retiring after twenty-five years of teaching kindergarten children in Sunday School. At the banquet many words of appreciation and praise were spoken concerning her fine, dedicated teaching.

When it came her turn to respond, in three minutes, as the Spirit spoke through her, she preached one of the most eloquent sermons.

> She said, "All these years the children have been teaching me about Jesus. He's real to them, and they made Him more real to me than I would have felt possible twenty-five years ago.

> Her eyes were twinkling, "For instance, I remember a little boy who burst out with, 'If Jesus came running through that door now, I'd run right up and hug Him.'"

> "I owe such a great deal to the children..." As she sat down, the people present no longer thought of her, but their eyes and attention were on Jesus.

Where the Holy Spirit is allowed to do His work, Jesus Christ will be glorified and others will be drawn to Him.

Oh, that we might become better acquainted with the Holy Spirit so that our lives might truly fulfill their divine purpose and glorify Jesus Christ! This is my prayer for you.

2. THE HOLY SPIRIT IS A GIFT

The Holy Spirit is a gift. Jesus said, *"I will not leave you orphans" (John 14:18, Swedish Translation).* we have not been abandoned. Just as earthly fathers love to give gifts to their children, so Jesus said, the Heavenly Father delights in giving good gifts to us. And according to Luke 11:13, the most special gift that God has for each of His children is the Holy Spirit. Why is the Holy Spirit the choice gift? Because when we have the Holy Spirit all the resources of God become available to us.

3. THE HOLY SPIRIT IS A POWER

Not only is the Holy Spirit a person. Not only is He the choice gift. **But He is the power of God that we must have in our lives.**
You are the temple of the Living God (I Corinthians 6:19-20). The Holy Spirit lives within the temple. And because He lives within you, all the resources and power that you need to stop feeling inferior and become an important person are inside of you. All the resources to overcome hate with love are within you. All the power to be released and set free is within you. It is the power of the Holy Spirit. Yes, *"Greater is he that is in you than he that is in the world" (I John 4:4).*

HOW TO TAP INTO THE POWER OF GOD

There is no substitute for the real thing. Early knowledge and education, no matter how fine and refined, will not make "greater works than these" happen through your life. Church growth conferences, as enlightening as they can be, will not make dead churches come alive. Programs, no matter how well thought out, will not make it happen in your church. **We simply cannot do God's work effectively without the power of the Holy Spirit.**
In Acts 8 we read about Philip, a deacon or what I call a lay pastor, who went down with the power of God within him to preach in Samaria. Wondrous miracles and signs happened. Multitudes were baptized into the Christian faith. The Kingdom of God was winning out over the kingdom of darkness. Sickness and sin were being vanquished.
Right in the middle of all this, Simon, one of the leaders in that community, became extremely interested in what he saw and wanted to have this great power. He offered the apostles money if only they would give to him this power. Peter answered, *"May*

your money perish with you, because you thought you could buy the gift of God with money!" (Acts 8:20, NIV).

There is no substitute for the power of God. It is something we've got to have. And there is no shortcut to getting the power of God. We can't buy it, as Simon learned, but it is our gift.

How do you tap into the power? As I am writing this in my office at New Hope Community Church I can look out the window and see large power lines that run along the edge of our property. Those power lines carry the power to light up thousands of homes in our area plus one of the city's major hospitals. There is enormous power in those lines. They remind me of what Maurice Berquist, author of the book *The Miracle and Power of Blessing* calls the parallel principle. If you pull a copper wire parallel to these overhead wires you get a transfer of power. Even though the second wire is not touching the overhead wire. Even though it is not connected to anything like a generator or dynamo, power will come into it just as soon as it gets parallel. There is a transfer of power that takes place.

When I heard this I thought about how that God is the source of all the power we need. The Holy Spirit is the power line and when we get out lives lined up parallel to God's will for our lives, the power begins to be transferred into and through our lives.

> The power to love without limit
> The power to fulfill our clear-cut vision
> The power to live clean in an unclean world
> The power to create God's world where we live
> The power to achieve great things for God
> The power to do "greater things than these"

When it comes to tapping into the power of God there are three key words that have opened the door for me personally into living in the power of the Spirit. These words are **filled, fellowship, and flow.** These are like stairsteps in that the first step is to be filled with the Spirit. The second step is to learn how to fellowship with the Spirit. Then, the third step is to flow in the Spirit. In II Corinthians 3:8 this question is asked: *"Will not the ministry of the Spirit be even more glorious?"* I can testify that ministry in the Spirit is a wonderful, glorious experience.

STEP ONE - BE FILLED WITH THE SPIRIT

Every Christian needs to know and experience what it is to be filled with the Holy Spirit. As we read through the Book of Acts, believers were first filled with the Spirit, then the ministry of God began to really happen through their lives. It is a Spirit-filled person that God can use to His glory. It is the Spirit-filled church that God can use to do extraordinary things.

In Ephesians 5:18 we read these words, *"Be not drunk with wine wherein is excess but be ye filled with the Holy Spirit" (KJ)*. What is characteristic of people under the influence of alcohol that is also characteristic of people filled with the Holy Spirit? They have less control of themselves and are under the control of something else. The big question is, who is going to be in charge? As someone has so appropriately put it, **"Jesus must be Lord of all or He will not be Lord at all."**

Before we can be filled with the Holy Spirit we must empty ourselves of everything foreign to God's will. Let's say that the Holy Spirit is the pitcher of water and we are the glass. The glass cannot be filled clear up with water until it is first emptied of everything else.

The one condition that you must meet to be filled with the Holy Spirit is described in Romans 12:1 in these words: *"I beseech you therefore, brethren, by the mercies of God, that ye present your bodies a living sacrifice, holy, acceptable unto God, which is your reasonable service" (KJ)*.

The word "present" can also be translated "yield." Picture in your mind a yield right-of-way sign on the highway. What does it mean? It means that you yield to oncoming traffic. The moment has come for you to put up the yield right-of-way sign in your life, to stop resisting and to yield it all to Him. Open up the secret rooms in the house of your life. Let the Holy Spirit of God take a clean sweep in your life and make you clean through and through (see Acts 15:8-9).

The greatest act of love you can give to God is to surrender to Him your total self for the carrying out of His purposes on this earth. I used to think that consecration was telling God all the good things I was going to do for Him. But I've learned that it is signing my name to a blank sheet of paper and then as we go along God fills in the details. My job is to keep saying, **"Yes, Lord, yes."**

The Spirit-filled life can be yours. Jesus said, *"Blessed are they that hunger and thirst after righteousness for they shall be filled"* *(Matthew 5:6)*.

STEP TWO - FELLOWSHIP WITH THE HOLY SPIRIT

In II Corinthians 13:14 we read, *"May the grace of the Lord Jesus Christ, and the love of God, and the fellowship of the Holy Spirit be with you all" (NIV)*. I have experienced the grace of the Lord Jesus Christ since my spiritual birth at the age of 15. I have enjoyed the love of God for 31 years since then. I experienced the filling of the Holy Spirit in my seminary days. But only the last three years have I begun to know **the joy of fellowshipping with the Holy Spirit.**

This new relationship began with a deep thirst inside of me really to know God and to have His power flowing through my life. As the ministry at New Hope Community Church has abounded in growth, an overwhelming realization has come to me that as Senior Pastor I cannot be successful in leading this church without daily help from Someone greater than I am. With success comes new and bigger problems to solve.

By meeting God the first thing in the morning for an extended period of time and learning to fellowship with the Holy Spirit on a heart-to-heart basis, I have found the Holy Spirit to be the missing connection that I have been looking for all these years. Jesus said it in a parable: He is the vine and we are the branches and therefore, *"Without me ye can do nothing" (John 15:5)*.

It's true. Without Him we cannot do the work of ministry. It just will not happen. The complexity, the problems, the depth of pain and extent of brokenness in people's lives today cannot be helped, changed and healed except as we become the instrument for the transforming power of God. The Holy Spirit is the missing connection that hooks our minds and hearts up to God's power.

Through fellowship with the Holy Spirit you can be connected. Jesus said, *"I am the vine, ye are the branches, He that abideth in me, and I in him, the same bringeth forth much fruit" (John 15:5, KJV)*. As you learn to fellowship with the Holy Spirit, your life will be fruitful because you're going to be connected to the living Lord.

With the outside pressures each of us face in an average day, we need a strength on the inside. I have found the secret. With this secret you can, no matter what your vocation may be, face anything with confidence.

I have a heart for people in business today. It seems there are so many pitfalls today lurking in the shadows in the business world. To be successful in business you need an inner strength.

To be a successful pastor or Christian worker you need an inner strength. To fulfill your calling to be an effective witness in an unclean world, you need inner strength. Attendance at Sunday worship, or weekly Bible study, although a great addition of strength, is not enough. Where do we get this inner bracing, this inner strength?

The Apostle Paul knew the answer as he prayed for the church and its leaders at Ephesus that, *"out of his glorious riches he may strengthen you with power through his spirit in your inner being" (Ephesians 3:16, NIV).* **I have discovered that as I fellowship with the Holy Spirit I am strengthened on the inside.** Thank God for the "Paraclete," the Holy Spirit, who is the strength of God within us.

By fellowshipping with the Holy Spirit we are prepared for the day. In Philippians 2:1 we read these words, *"...if any fellowship with the Spirit..."* Out of that fellowship will flow winning attitudes, right motivations and good actions towards others which will result in successful living. **Fellowship with the Holy Spirit is the key for you to make each day a special day.**

In fellowship with the Holy Spirit our minds are freed from anxieties, and cleansed from pollution. Our mental wanderings become singleness of mind to will and do what God wants. In this renewing of our mind we are transformed and set free from this polluted world to be at one with God so that His creative ideas may flow through our lives. My personal discovery has been that as I fellowship with the Holy Spirit my creativity comes alive and God's ideas are released into my mind.

Through fellowship with the Holy Spirit came my vision to build a church of 15,000 by 1990. As I continue to fellowship with the Holy Spirit the details of that vision are being unfolded and becoming a reality.

Last year as I fellowshipped with the Holy Spirit, our prayer ministry at New Hope Community Church was conceived. These morning prayer times have become the power center for all the ministries of New Hope Community Church. I'll tell you more about this in the next chapter. It was as I fellowshipped with the Holy Spirit that the concept of our new 3000-seat sanctuary, now completed, was created.

In my daily fellowship with the Holy Spirit right now, we are talking together about five major things to come in the ministry of New Hope Community Church.

To fellowship with the Holy Spirit you must get it straight as to who is in charge. **The Holy Spirit is my senior partner.** I am the junior partner. I am dependent upon the Lord for strength and direction. My part is to say yes, Lord, yes.

As I fellowship with the Holy Spirit, I have learned that I can ask for wisdom. *"If any of you lack wisdom, he should ask God, who gives genmerously to all..." (James 1:5, NIV).* If you need wisdom in knowing how to handle your teenager, fellowship with the Holy Spirit and ask for that wisdom and receive it. Do you need wisdom in a major business decision? Fellowship with the Holy Spirit and ask for it and receive it. Wait on the Lord and He will direct your path.

I have been absolutely amazed at how beautifully God has given the answers to very complex problems as I have fellowshipped with the Holy Spirit.

I am learning that my Helper, **the Holy Spirit, is interested in every detail of my life.** Weekly I have the awesome responsibility of preparing sermons, not only for a large congregation but for mailing distribution to thousands more.

Invariably as I am preparing my sermon, to my mind will come an illustration or a principle that I have at some time filed away somewhere. If I were looking for the missing data by myself, it would take hours, maybe days, but my Helper, the Holy Spirit, again and again has taken me right to where I can lay my hands on the needed material. My friend and senior partner saves me much valuable time.

Before learning to fellowship with the Holy Spirit, I would often go home after preaching three times on Sunday morning and be at the lowest point of my life emotionally. Let me tell you how I have overcome that. Before going to preach the three morning services, I say, "Holy Spirit, this is your sermon. I am your instrument. Let's go do your work." Then afterwards, I thank the Holy Spirit and leave the outcome of that message in His hands. Then I don't get all down on myself for not doing it just the right way.

In the Holy Spirit we have a marvelous transportation system. Every civilization has been known by its transportation system. One of the keys to the prosperity we enjoy in America is our excellent systems of transportation. They are the greatest in the history of the world. but as Christians, we have a yet greater transportation system. He is the One and only Holy Spirit of God, who not only bears witness with our hearts that we are the children of God but who carries back and forth from our hearts to God's heart those things that need to be communicated.

In Romans 8:26-27 we are given this truth: *"In the same way, the Spirit helps us in our weakness. We do not know how we ought to pray, but the spirit himself intercedes for us with groans that words cannot express. And he who searches our hearts knows the mind of the Spirit, because the Spirit intercedes for the saints in accordance with God's will" (NIV).*

Things are going on inside of us that we don't even understand, that we can't put into words. The Spirit of God, if we fellowship with Him, communicates that for us to God the Father. Back to us comes the help and answer that we need. Continually the Holy Spirit meets our greatest need by transporting into us the love of God. *"God has poured out his love into our hearts by the Holy Spirit, whom he has given us" (Romans 5:5, NIV).* Thank God for the Holy Spirit who is our transportation system.

In fellowship with the Holy Spirit there is created a spiritual sensitivity which can be described as an awareness of our dependency on the Lord. This dependency upon the Lord opens the windows of heaven for all the good things of God to come into our lives.

As you fellowship with God's Spirit, your life will begin to fulfill its purpose and to reflect the glory of God. After all, we were created to glorify God. In fellowship with the Holy Spirit this marvelous mystery begins to unfold. We feel an openness and freedom in the Lord that, when lived out in daily life, becomes openness and freedom with other people. Then we no longer relate to others out of fear but out of the love and a sound mind that God is pouring into our lives (II Timothy 1:7). When this happens, we fulfill the words of II Chronicles 3:18 and *"reflect the Lord's glory" (NIV)*. And the more a person fellowships with the Holy Spirit, the more his or her life becomes a reflection of the glory of the Lord.

You can actually stop living on the rollercoaster of circumstances and live in the freedom and glory that comes through daily fellowship with the One who is within you, the Holy Spirit. We see this illustrated in the life of Stephen, a lay leader in the early church. Stephen was filled with the Holy Spirit and lived in daily fellowship with the Holy Spirit. When the circumstances were terrible and he faced death, even his enemies testified afterward that his face shown with the glory of the Lord (see Acts 6:15). The more their hatred was spewed out against Stephen, the more the fellowship with the Holy Spirit and supernatural love and forgiveness flowed through his life. And standing by watching from a distance was one Saul of Tarsus in whose hardened heart was planted the unforgettable witness of perfect love.

STEP THREE - FLOW IN THE SPIRIT

Out of being filled with the Holy Spirit and out of daily fellowshipping with Him comes the sensitivity and obedience to flow with the Holy Spirit. What does it mean to flow with the Holy Spirit?

The Holy Spirit is a gentleman. When Jesus was baptized, the dove, which was a symbol for the Spirit, descended upon Him. The dove is a gentle bird. The Holy Spirit is the perfect gentleman. He will not force Himself nor will He force the will of God on anyone. God respects the free will that He gave us when He created us.

The Scriptures teach us that we must be careful not to resist or grieve the Spirit. *"Do not put out the Spirit's fire" (I Thessalonians 5:19, NIV).* Or, as the Living Bible puts it, *"Do not smother the Holy Spirit."* In Ephesians 4:30 we read: *"And do not grieve the Holy Spirit of God, with whom you were sealed for the day of re-*

demption." To flow with the Spirit means not to resist the Spirit in any way but to cooperate with the Spirit of God in doing His ministry. Cooperation means doing everything on your part to obey the Holy Spirit and carry out in this joint operation what He wants you to do. The greatest program a church can have both for outreach and ministry to each other, is for its members to learn to flow with the Spirit and do as the Spirit directs. When the Holy Spirit lays someone on your heart, respond by phoning and encouraging that person.

The members of the early church were successful according to the history recorded in the Book of Acts, because they flowed with the Spirit. In chapter two of Acts we see that after they were filled with the Holy Spirit they flowed with the Spirit and scattered throughout Jerusalem gossiping with overflowing enthusiasm what Jesus had done in their lives. The result was a great in-gathering as, flowing with the Holy Spirit, Peter preached his famous sermon. On that very day 3000 were added to the church. Things really begin to happen when God's people start flowing in the Spirit.

In Acts 3 we see Peter and John going up to the Temple where they were approached by a crippled man begging for money. Flowing in the Spirit, they did not give him what he asked but gave him something much greater. By the power of God flowing through Peter and John, the crippled man jumped to his feet and began to walk. The success and explosion of the early church is a direct result of flowing in the Spirit, obeying God rather than man.

In Acts 5 we see a vivid illustration of what happens when people resist the Holy Spirit. The not flowing, the resisting, the lying to the Holy Spirit was the undoing of Ananias and Sapphira. Resisting the Holy Spirit in any shape or form is the undoing not only of the individual Christian life but of the mighty work that God wants to do in our churches. You can tap into the power of God if you can answer these three questions in the affirmative. (1) **Have you been filled with the Holy Spirit?** (2) **Are you fellowshipping with the Holy Spirit?** (3) **Are you flowing with the Holy Spirit?**

My own testimony is that I am learning how to flow with the Holy Spirit. It's coming out of my being filled with the Holy Spirit and my learning daily to fellowship with the Holy Spirit. And it's coming out of my learning to be sensitive to the guidance and directives of the Holy Spirit by saying, **"Yes, Lord, yes"**.

Since I have been learning to flow with the Spirit, many times when I preach, no matter what I preach on, when I come to the end of the message and speak the words of faith, people stand up and receive Christ's salvation flow. Flowing in the Spirit, I begin to speak the Lord's faith, and healings take place. Flowing in the Spirit, I've seen marvelous church growth taking place in our fellowship.

Make this contemporary marvelous song your song:

> "I'll say, 'Yes, Lord, yes'
> To Your will and to Your way.
> I'll say, 'Yes, Lord, yes';
> I will trust You and obey.
> When Your Spirit speaks to me,
> With my whole heart I'll agree,
> And my answer will be,
> 'Yes, Lord, yes!' "
> -Words and music by Lynn Keesecker

PART I - POWER

CHAPTER 3 - POWER
OF PRAYER

Six-year-old Marvin was asked what makes boys good or bad. He answered: "Good boys say their prayers."

"That's right," said the interviewer. "Marvin, which prayers do you say?"

"That's the whole trouble," Marvin sighed, "I don't say any."

This is the testimony of not just a few among us, but most of us. It has been estimated that the average church member in America prays *less than 20 minutes a week.* My honest confession is that for years as a pastor I made the big mistake of getting along with a minimum amount of prayer instead of maximizing my ministry with prayer.

Prayer is the breadth and depth of a Christian life. Every study of growing churches reveals that the dynamic churches— where it's happening—have in common the fact that prayer has a central place in their ministry. No church can begin to accomplish what God is calling them to do without a power center of prayer. It's simple. You cannot do God's work without God. Yet, so many of us keep on trying to do it on our own.

I. THINGS REALLY BEGIN TO HAPPEN WHEN WE PRAY

As one reads the Book of Acts and traces the steps of those early disciples, he becomes aware right off the bat that to them praying was not something they might do but something they wanted to do. They recognized that they could not stand against their opposition and do the great work of ministry without tapping into God's power through prayer.

With their lives under threat of extermination if they continued to speak and teach in the name of Jesus, the disciples made their petition to the Lord in these words: *"Enable your servants to speak your word with great boldness. Stretch out your hand to heal and perform miraculous signs and wonders through the name of your holy servant, Jesus" (Acts 4:29-30, NIV).*

When they had prayed—their spirits touching God's Spirit—seven things happened:

1. The place was shaken
2. They were all filled with the Holy Spirit.
3. They spoke the Word of God with boldness.
4. There was a oneness of heart shared by all of those who had prayed together.
5. There was a sense of stewardship that everything belonged to God and should be used for helping each other.
6. They became winsome, attractive Christians.
7. They ministered with great power.
(Acts 4:31-33, NIV)

II. MULTIPLE BENEFITS COME INTO OUR LIVES FROM PRAYER

Through prayer we are connected to the power of God. Jesus said, *"Apart from me you can do nothing" (John 15:5, NIV).* But He also said, *"If you remain in me and my words remain in you, ask whatever you wish, and it will be given you" (v. 7).* It is prayer that connects us to the holy, all-powerful One, who is everything.

The first benefit of your being connected to God through prayer is that your life is going to be fruitful. As you practice the abiding principle your life will become productive (John 15:2, 8, 16).The desire to have your life really used by God is going to be fulfilled. God wants to answer your prayer but first you must make your request known to Him.

Recently I was thinking about the many benefits that have been flowing into my life as a result of my commitment to make prayer a top priority in my life. Here are a few of the benefits that I have been enjoying:

ASSURANCE that my clear-cut vision and goals for our church are exactly what God wants at this time.

STRENGTH and AWARENESS that He is with me helping me to live victoriously and to overcome the attacks of Satan.

CONFIDENCE that the promises I read in the Word of God are for me. Here's one the Lord gave to me in recent days, from Psalm 37:4: *"May he grant you your heart's desire and fulfill all your plans."*

WISDOM—Anybody who lives in a family and raises children needs wisdom beyond his own. There were times this week when I had to ask the Lord for wisdom in working with one of my children. The Bible promises in James 1:5—*"if any of you lack wisdom, he should ask God, who gives generously to all without finding fault, and it will be given to him."*

CORRECTION—When my behavior is not what it should be, then in prayer my spirit becomes humble and accepting of the correction of the Lord. This permits my growing into the name "Christian" to go on.

ATTITUDE—As I fellowship with the Lord, the negative is eliminated and my mind becomes clearly focused in on the positive. There is the renewing of my mind and spirit which is so important in order for me to be at my best (see Romans 12:2).

CLEANSING—There is the confession of any wrongdoing. This leads to forgiveness and fellowship with the Lord and fellow Christians (see I John 1:9).

PEACE—No matter what goes wrong or what happens I have an inner peace that comes from knowing Jesus is with me.

LOVE—There is no greater feeling in all the world than knowing that I am loved by God. This frees me so that, through the power of the Spirit within, I can really receive love and give love.

JOY—The joy of the Lord is my strength.

In the time of prayer I've found this verse in Psalm 17:15 (LB) to be my testimony: *"But as for me, my contentment is not in wealth but in seeing you and knowing all is well between us. And when I awake in heaven, I will be fully satisfied, for I will see you face to face."* THERE'S NOTHING GREATER THAN KNOWING GOD AND FELLOWSHIPPING WITH HIM.

III. MAKE PRAYER A TOP PRIORITY

Everyone knows that prayer is a good thing. We all know that we should pray. Why is it that a lot of us don't? We mean to but somehow we never quite get around to it. I can only give you my own testimony. It is this: prayer did not really characterize my life until I got so hungry and thirsty for more of God that I started getting up an hour early every morning to spend that special time with God in prayer. I admit to you that it was tough, but now it has become the most blessed hour of my day.

In Exodus 16 we read about a miraculous experience of the children of Israel. After they had been delivered across the Red Sea and were out in the wilderness, they were in need. God had a very special way of supplying their need. Each morning when they got up there was a manna that tasted like a honey bread on the ground. They were told to gather fresh every morning what they needed for that day. If they tried to gather more than one day's supply, they found that it would rot. However, on the sixth day they could gather two day's supply, so that they would not work on the Sabbath, and it would not rot.

God provided this for them every day of the forty years that they were wandering around in the wilderness before entering the Promised Land of Canaan where there was milk and honey.

It took quite a while for the children of Israel to get through their heads but eventually they learned to trust God and to know that every morning He would supply their daily need. They would go out and meet God in the morning and He would give them their daily bread.

Make it a habit to ask God for your daily bread every morning in prayer. The deepest need in your life, which is spiritual, will then be supplied by the presence and power and blessings of Almighty God.

Do you know what is the greatest lesson you could ever learn? Every sin that has ever been committed on the earth—think about how much destruction that is—has been the result of either not knowing or not practicing this important lesson.

Whenever people miss this lesson, they repeatedly get themselves into deep waters of trouble. What is this important lesson taught to us in John 15 when Jesus said, *"I am the vine; you are the branches."*? It is this: DEPEND ON THE LORD!

Depending on the Lord is the opposite of the "pride" that the Scriptures teach us "goes before a fall" (Proverbs 16:18). Jesus said, *"Without me you can do nothing."* In the context of this fifteenth chapter of John, Jesus taught us the "abiding principle." We are to abide in Jesus like the branches abide in the vine, depending upon the Lord. It is in Christ that we come alive and become fruitful and productive. Abiding, for me, means meeting God in a divine appointment the first thing every morning and spending the time with Him until we have talked it all over. Out of my abiding prayer time flows the strength of my day and the power to lead the rapidly increasing church that I pastor.

The battles we face in a particular day are either won or lost depending upon whether or not we meet God the first thing in the morning. When we meet our Lord in the morning we become "more than conquerors through Him who loved us" (Romans 8:37, NIV).

At New Hope Community Church we make prayer a top priority in the life of the church. Every morning we have a prayer hour from 6:30 to 7:30. In our messages and publications we emphasize this as being central to all of our ministries.

A second way we make prayer a priority is, in our Tender Loving Care groups, we teach our leadership to gather the people in a prayer circle.

The third way we make prayer a priority is that in every one of our services we have a Garden of Prayer. People are invited to the front to kneel in prayer and to be prayed for by one of our Lay Pastors.

The fourth way we make prayer a top priority is that pastors and leaders of the church model prayer as a way of life.

IV. HOW DO YOU PRAY?

The other day someone expressed, really, the desire of all of our hearts when he asked me this question: "Pastor, how do you pray?" Our Lord Jesus responded to that same question from His disciples by giving to us the model prayer—The Lord's Prayer.(Luke 11:1-4). A study of The Lord's prayer reveals a five point outline that I teach our people as five fingers on the hand that moves with God.

In my own personal prayer life I used to run out of anything to say after two or three minutes. Now with this outline, following the five main points of The Lord's Prayer, I find that I can not only pray for an hour at a time but sometimes much longer. As I have shared this simple five finger outline, God has used it to teach people to break through in a whole new way in their prayer life. Here is the outline for you to benefit from:

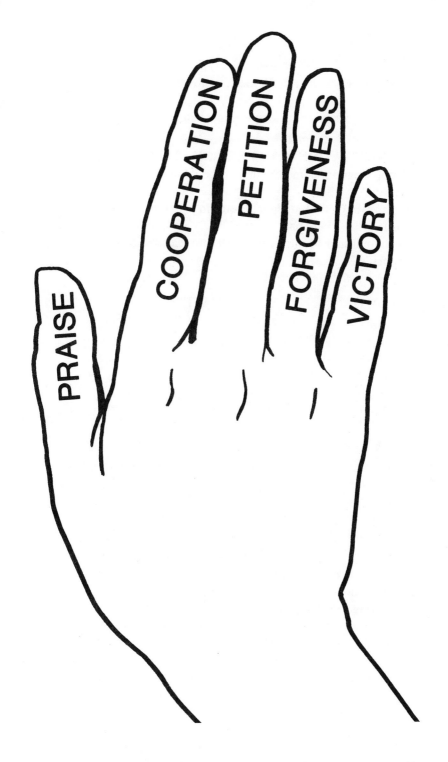

1. PRAISE—THE TUNING-IN STEP
"Our Father which art in Heaven, hallowed be Your Name."
a. Who He is.
b. What He has done in scripture and in our lives. (James 1:17)

2. COOPERATION—CONNECTION STEP
"Your kingdom come, Your will be done on earth as it is in Heaven."
a. Pray for God's kingdom to come in your city, in your church and family—every part of your life.
b. Submit and fit into God's will and leadership in your life (Romans 12:1).

3. PETITION—THE RECEIVING STEP
"Give us this day our daily bread,"
a. Concerns (Philippians 4:4-7)
b. Intercession
c. Asking for wisdom (James 1:5)
d. Praying for and receiving prosperity (III John 2)
e. Be specific. Detail in steps what you are asking for.

4. FORGIVENESS—THE HEALING STEP
"And forgive us our sins as we forgive those who sinned against us."
a. Confession and cleansing (I John 1:9)
b. Forgiving and blessing those who have wronged you. (Hebrews 12:15; James 3)

5. VICTORY—The Can Do Step
"Lead us not into temptation but deliver us from evil, for Thine is the kingdom, the power and the glory—forever."
a. Ask for and claim victory over temptation (James 4:7-8).
b. In Jesus' name claim deliverance and protection from Satan's attacks (I John 4:4).
c. Be glorified in my life.
d. Make positive affirmations (Philippians 4:13).

V. TEN FURTHER HELPS FOR EFFECTIVE PRAYING

HELP NO 1 - PRAISE AND WORSHIP

How good God is. His mercies are everlasting. I praise and thank God for who He is. You learn to do this by reading the Psalms, which record the prayers of praise. The reason we are to praise the Lord is that our ministry is to be first unto the Lord. (For example see Psalm 103)

I spend time praising God the Father, Jesus the Son, and I praise my companion and helper, the Holy Spirit.

Then I thank God for His constant flow of good gifts into my life. We have all received of His richness and generous gifts. We are a blessed people. Count your blessings, name them one by one, and it will surprise you what the Lord has done.

Sometimes when I am sure that no one else is around, I like to sing my praises and thanksgiving to the Lord.

HELP NO. 2—COME CLEAN BEFORE THE LORD

Every morning when I get up, I brush my teeth, shave, take a shower. What am I doing? I am cleaning up to get a clean start on a new day.

This is exactly what we need to do spiritually. We come before the Lord in His holy presence, we open up in honesty and confession. We breathe out any wrong attitudes. We breathe out any wrong motives. We confess any and all unforgiven sin and we breathe in God's forgiveness and cleansing. We get cleaned up to get a fresh new start. God specializes in brand new beginnings.

In prayer make these words the communication from your heart to God: *"Let the words of my mouth and meditation of my heart be acceptable in thy sight, O Lord, my strength, and my redeemer" (Psalm 19:14, KJ).*

My prayer is that I will become in spirit and attitude and action more and more like my Lord Jesus. That God's life will flow through me. I want to be His instrument for healing and salvation to others. But for God to use me, I must keep cleaned up.

HELP NO. 3—CONCERN

I share with the Lord each of the concerns that I have in my life. This may be something that is going on with one of our children. It can be anything that is causing me anxiety. Often it is the impossible projects that I am working on. Each day I go through the projects step by step with my heavenly Father and we refine the steps toward the great achievement for God.

For example, when new ministries are placed on the planning board at New Hope Community Church, each morning in my concern time I talk to the Lord about the kind of person we are looking for to lead these new ministries.

I can remember during the launching of building our 3000-seat auditorium of having to make weighty decisions every day. I talked over the concerns of this building project each morning with my heavenly Father.

By the time I talked through each concern with my Lord, Friend, and Senior Partner, the muscles in my body, instead of being tight, are relaxed and at ease. A confidence, assurance, and a strength that is a gift from God had come into my being.

HELP NO. 4—INTERCESSION

I intercede to God for the reaching of 10,000 people for Christ in Portland, Oregon. I intercede that salvation will flow in our ministry at New Hope. I intercede that healing will flow through our ministry. I intercede for each of our staff pastors, their spouses, and families. I intercede for the different need-meeting ministries at New Hope Community Church. I intercede for the business people in my church praying they will be prosperous in their businesses. I intercede to God for our young people that they will be called of God to ministry and respond to that call. I intercede for any of our ministries that are weak, that they will become strong. I intercede for our 525 Lay Pastors who lead more than 500 TLC Groups.

HELP NO. 5—PRAY THROUGH MY DAY

In conversation with the Lord, I go through the different appointments I am going to have in the day.

I take God into each of these appointments, asking for His help, guidance and blessing. I ask that I will be a channel through which His love flows, touches, heals, and lifts other people's lives. I ask for wisdom for the situation where I know I don't have the answers. Having prayed through every appointment in my day from morning to evening, I am prepared for my day with Jesus as my leader. I am aware that He is with me and will use me to do and accomplish His purposes. What a wonderful way to make the most of a day!

HELP NO. 6—THE HOLY SPIRIT IS OUR TRANSPORTATION SYSTEM

He carries from my heart the messages to God. And He carries back from God exactly what I need in my life for the day. I love the Holy Spirit. He makes Jesus so close to me and me so close to Jesus.

As we have communion together, any of those things that I have not covered in prayer to this point are shared. Even those things that I cannot put into words are communicated through the language of the Spirit (see Romans 8:26-27). As I commune with God in this holy fellowship, the fruits of the Spirit are poured into my life: love, joy, peace, patience, kindness, goodness, faithfulness, gentleness and self control (see Galatians 5:22). These become dominant in and through my life because I have become a channel through which the Holy Spirit can communicate the life of Jesus.

HELP NO. 7 —BE SPECIFIC

Praying in generalities will not get anything accomplished. How can you even know when your prayers are answered if you just pray in vague, undefined terms? We need to zero in on exactly what it is that we want God to do for us.

When Jesus was walking down the road out of Jericho and Bartimaeus came wobbling to him through the crowds, Jesus asked him, *"What do you want? (see Mark 10:46-52).* Jesus wanted the man to tell Him exactly what it was he wanted.

For a long time I have had the desire in my heart for a three-piece black silk suit, custom made to fit. So I started talking to my heavenly Father about this very detailed request. One of the details was that it had to be at a price I could afford.

A couple of months after I started praying this specific prayer, I had the privilege of taking a trip to Korea and while there I went shopping. One morning I walked into a tailor shop and met the head man named Johnny. There hanging on the wall I noticed the most beautiful black silk material. I asked him how much he would charge to make me a three-piece suit. He said, "Because you're the first customer for the day, I want to give you a good deal. I'll make you that custom black suit for $100." One year later I am still enjoying the beautiful custom black suit that is my answer to prayer.

Your heavenly Father is interested in every detail of your life. I'll bet that you cannot tell me how many hairs you have on your head. Do you know that your heavenly Father knows the exact number of hairs that you have on your head? That's not all He knows. He knows every need you have. But you have not because you ask not in detail.

HELP NO. 8—BE PERSISTENT

Should we keep repeating the same request to the Lord? Jesus answered this question by saying, *"Ask and it will be given to you; seek and you will find; knock and the door will be opened to you"* *(Luke 11:9, NIV).*

Preceding this verse that teaches the persistence principle, Jesus illustrates the teaching: There was a man who went late at night to his neighbor's house because he needed food to feed unexpected guests. The friend was asleep but because the man persisted in knocking, the friend got up and came to the door and answered his request.

I don't know about your children, but my children know that persistence pays off. With our heavenly Father, we are to keep on asking, seeking, knocking, as our children do with us, until we either have the assurance in our heart that it's going to be answered or the answer has come.

Right now I am continuing to take a number of requests to the Lord on a daily basis. I am discovering that as I continue to talk to God about a request on a daily basis, it is clarified and broken down into manageable steps. The Lord and I are working together on fulfilling the request. It is in prayer that I am learning to pace myself and adjust to God's perfect timing.

HELP NO. 9—LEARN TO PRAY THROUGH

We are all a part of the now generation. We have instant potatoes, instant TV dinners, instant entertainment, and instant gratification. In order to pray through you have to spend a lot of time with God.

Most of the difficulties that we get ourselves into are a result of charging ahead without taking time to really pray through and get God's direction of our lives.

As I became aware of this I decided to commit our church to a daily prayer time on a regular basis. Our busy people must learn to take the time to pray through. I also made a commitment in my own life to pray an hour the first thing every morning, seeking, waiting before the Lord, spending the time with Him to really know Him. The better we know Him, the more we know exactly what He wants us to do.

HELP NO. 10—POSITIVE PRAYERS

So many times people short circuit their own prayer request by the feeble, unbelieving way they pray., By the very timid, half-hearted way they speak you can tell that they don't really expect anything to happen, and consequently it doesn't. We are to pray in faith, believing.

In Ephesians 3:20, we read the think-ask principle: *"Now unto him that is able to do exceeding abundantly above all that we ask or think, according to the power that worketh in us, unto Him be glory"* (KJ) This teaches that we are not only to ask in faith, believing, but we are to cooperate with that request by thinking positive, expecting thoughts about the request.

When it comes to getting our prayers answered, asking and thinking are two sides of the same coin. We are to ask positively and we are to think positively. Asking positively and thinking positively is cooperating with God to bring the answer we've been seeking. To have God's answers in our life we must cooperate with the power of God.

VI. FOUR KINDS OF PRAYER THAT GOD WANTS TO TEACH US IN ORDER TO RELEASE SIGNS AND WONDERS

Where God's power is flowing as it was in the early church there will be *"signs and wonders" (see Acts 2:22; Acts 3:9; Acts 4:16; Acts 4:21; Acts 4:31; Acts 5:12; Acts 6:8; Acts 8:17; Acts 15:8-9)*.

1. PRAYER AND FASTING—Some sicknesses, disease, oppression, depression, habits and obsession can only be removed through prayer and fasting.

The disciples once asked Jesus why they could not cast out the devil from a possessed boy. Jesus answered, *"Howbeit this kind goeth not out but by prayer and fasting" (see Matthew 17:19-21, KJ)*. Some things are so difficult that they cannot happen except through prayer and fasting.

A talented young man who's a personal friend of mine has felt led and called of God to be a positive motivator to Christian people. He has been preparing himself and seeking God's direction in getting started.

A couple of months ago he seemed to be up against a brick wall. Nothing was opening up for him until he prayed and fasted for a week. Then just like the Red Sea parted, the doors began to open for him, one by one. His break-through began with prayer and fasting.

2. HEALING PRAYERS—*"Jesus Christ is the same yesterday and today and forever" (Hebrews 13:8)*. Just as He healed people back then, people are healed today, through the power of the Holy Spirit in the name of Jesus, in a praying church. Our church is a healing fellowship. We practice James 5:16, *"Confess your faults one to another, and pray one for another that ye may be healed" (KJ)*.

At each of our services we have a time we call the Garden of Prayer. People come forward and kneel and Lay Pastors come in love and gently touch them in healing prayers. Miracles of healing happen.

In our Tender Loving Care groups that gather throughout our metropolitan area all times of the day, every day of the week, people become a healing fellowship to one another in the name of Jesus. As they confess their faults and needs, they respond in love by praying for one another and healing happens. Did Jesus not tell us that whatsoever we would bind on earth would be bound in heaven and whatsoever we would loose on earth would be loosed in heaven? He has given us the authority to be instruments of His healing in each other's lives (see Matthew 16:25).

3. INTERCESSORY PRAYER—An intercessor is a person who stands beween God and an urgent need and pleads to God for that need. Abraham interceded for his nephew, Lot, when God was going to destroy the city of Sodom and Gomorrah. God heard Abraham's cry and saved Lot.

Each morning in my divine appointment with God, I intercede for all the ministers on my pastoral team. I intercede for my Lay Pastors. I intercede for my people. I intercede for the lost people in Portland, Oregon. I intercede that the churches in my city will be blessed of God.

I remember one week when the load was particularly heavy for me as the senior pastor. Having spent time in prayer and having sought counsel from leaders, I had to make some lonely and tough decisions.

Early Saturday morning, however, while walking with my best friend and wife, Margi, I told her how free I felt. Like I didn't have a care in the world. Then I said, "I believe that our people have been interceding for me."

The next day I found out that at 11:30 Friday night, at our prayer night, a large number of people interceded for their senior pastor before the Lord. WE REALLY DO NEED EACH OTHER'S PRAYERS.

4. AGREEING PRAYER—Agreeing prayer may be likened to strings that are braided together. Alone they can be broken but bound together they gain an unbreakable strength.

Jesus said: *"If two of you shall agree on earth as touching any-*

thing that they shall ask, it shall be done for them of my Father which is in heaven" (Matthew 18:19, KJ). Jesus also promised that agreeing prayer would not only provide the strength that comes from unity, but that He would add His strength and power to that by being there (see Matthew 18:20).

In Acts 12 we see that the church interceded in agreeing prayer for Peter, who was imprisoned and facing death. As the church, bound together and interceding, prayed, the hand of God was moved and Peter was miraculously freed from prison.

At New Hope Community Church I continually call the whole church to intercede in agreeing prayer for the vision and dream that God has given us to reach 10,000 people in Portland, Oregon by the year 2000. We are bound together and interceding to God for the answer to this prayer.

While in Korea I had the privilege of attending the Friday all-night prayer meeting with 10,000 other people in Dr. Paul Cho's church. At one point, Dr. Cho stood up and introduced the foreign visitors in the balcony where I was sitting. He said, "Now these church leaders are here because they want to be greatly used of God. Let's all, in agreeing prayer, intercede for them and pray for their filling of the Holy Spirit."

I wish you could have seen those 10,000 Koreans raise their hands to heaven, direct their prayers towards us, and in one voice pray for us. Suddenly people all around me began to experience the force and power of God. I can testify that my own heart and life was deeply touched by the power of God. I had an overwhelming sense of being filled with the Spirit of God. Is there anything greater than to be in His presence and to be at one with God?

LET US PRAY.

PART I - POWER

CHAPTER 4 - POWER OF LOVE

Yesterday an apartment manager called our home to tell us that a young lady who had attended our church a few times had committed suicide. She had been alone, dead, in her apartment for seven days before her body was discovered. Neighbors told the police that before the apartment next door had become silent, they had heard the young lady crying for days.

What can heal our hurts? What can put lives shattered into a million pieces back together again? What can make us feel good about ourselves? In our society multitudes are perishing from a variety of diseases of mind, body, and soul. Many of these diseases result from a lack of love in their lives. **There is no substitute for love. What our world needs now is what each of us need. It is love!**

Back in the early sixties when I was a seminary student the great theologian, Karl Barth, came to this country to lecture at a Chicago university. He was one of the great minds of our century. A reporter, interviewing him, asked, "Mr. Barth, what is the most profound thought you've ever had?"

Without hesitation Karl Barth said, "It was what my mother taught me in this little song, "Jesus loves me, this I know, for the Bible tells me so." The greatest thing in all the world is to receive God's *agape* love and become a transmitter of that love to others. According to I Corinthians 13, love is the greatest power.

On a cold, windy Sunday morning in Chicago with the chill factor 15 below zero, a little orphan boy, Ralph, walked four miles to church. His friend, Mr. Kennedy, greeted him as he came in the door, "Glad to see you, Ralph; sure is cold out there today."

With a smile Ralph said, "I sure did get cold walking this morning."

Surprised, the older man inquired, "You mean, Ralph, that you walked in this cold wind to church this morning?"

Ralph replied, "Yep, I didn't have money for bus fare."

"Well, how far did you walk, Ralph?"

"I walked four miles."

Mr. Kennedy asked Ralph, "How many churches did you pass along the way walking your four miles?"

Ralph thought for a moment. "I passed twenty-two churches."

Impressed, Mr. Kennedy said, "Ralph why did you pass twenty-two churches to come to this church on this cold morning?"

Ralph smiled a big Jimmy Carter smile and said, "Because I've discovered that here they love a fella like me."

Young or old, people will inconvenience themselves and go many miles to attend a church where they find love. It's not the size or the site that makes a church great, but it is the spirit of love. What the world needs now is love. And that's exactly what God has called us as members of the church to give to each other. And we are to keep extending the circle of love to those on the outside.

Someone asked me the other day what was the secret of the phenomenal success and growth of New Hope Community Church. I replied, "We practice many church growth principles which come out of the Book of Acts."

My friend pressed me a little further and said, "But what is the one thing that makes your church successful?" He was wanting to know some great big yet undiscovered secret.

I smiled at him and said, **"The secret of our growth is love."**

Here at New Hope Community Church we are learning how to love each other His way. This is the heartbeat of every truly successful church. Of all the things that can go on at a church, love is the greatest.

MAKE LOVE YOUR NUMBER ONE AIM
AND YOU WILL BE RIGHT ON TARGET

SIX THINGS YOU NEED TO KNOW ABOUT THE POWER OF LOVE

I. LOVE IS THE MOST POSITIVE FORCE IN THE WORLD
The great love chapter, I Corinthians 13, reveals many positive facts that you need to know about God's kind of love. It is:

PATIENT - "suffers long" (v. 4)
KIND - *"is kind" (v. 4)*
GENEROUS - *"envieth not" (v. 4)*
HUMBLE - *"is not puffed up" (v. 4)*
COURTEOUS - *is not rude (v. 5)*
UNSELFISH - *is not self-serving (v. 5)*
GOOD TEMPERED - *"is not easily provoked" (v. 5)*
GUILELESS - *thinks no evil (v. 5)*
SINCERE - *rejoices not in iniquity but rejoices in truth (v. 6)*
EDIFYING - *believes the best (v. 7)*
(I Corinthians 13)

A young lady came to me who was really down on her husband. For the first forty minutes she told me what a crummy husband she had and what a rotten deal it was being married to him. After I had all I could take, I decided to ask her a few questions.

I said, "Tell me, does your husband beat up on you?"

She acted like I had slapped her. She said, "No! he wouldn't do anything like that."

I said, "Does he gamble away the paycheck? Does he run around with women? Does he mistreat you or the kids?"

Each time she answered no, she got more indignant with me.

I said, "Well, is he a good father to your children?"

She said, "He's a wonderful father, you couldn't ask for a better father."

I persisted, "Is he kind and considerate to you?"

She smiled a little and said, "He's always kind and considerate of me." Then she said, "You know, he's not such a bad person after all: in fact, I'm a whole lot better off than most women." Then she smiled as if everything was all right, thanked me for all the good advice and left the office.

She had forgotten that love is a positive force. Love looks for and finds the best in the other person. In this negative world, how essential it is that we put to work the positive force of love in all our relationships. One of the key principles that we have practiced from day one at New Hope Community Church is the principle of showing our positive love for one another by edifying one another. In Romans 14:19 we read: *"Let us therefore make every effort to do what leads to peace and to mutual edification."* Then it goes on to say, *"Do not destroy the work of God for the sake of food"* *(NIV)*.

How many times in churches people destroy the flow of positive love over little dinky things which are not worth it. **Show me a church where they practice mutual edification and I'll show you a church where the power of love is in action and people will not only flock there but will stay there.** The way to build your church is to get into releasing the positive power of love that God has given you.

The Scriptures teach us: *"God is love" (I John 4:17). "The Word was made flesh" (John 1:14).* Jesus was both the message and the messenger of love sent to us from God. He came, bringing us all of God's love. His love is ours to receive. The moment we receive Jesus, all of the love of God is ours. Yes, love is our greatest possibility. Every time we choose to love we release the powerful force of God's love into our world.

II. LOVE IS A HEALING FORCE

"The Spirit of the Lord God is upon me, because the Lord has anointed me to bring good news to the suffering and afflicted. He has sent me to comfort the broken-hearted, to announce liberty to captives and to open the eyes of the blind. He has sent me to tell those who mourn that the time of God's favor to them has come, and the day of his wrath to their enemies. To all who mourn in Israel he will give Beauty for ashes; Joy instead of mourning; Praise instead of heaviness. For God has planted them like strong and graceful oaks for his own glory!" (Isaiah 61:1-3, LB).

This is a description of the healing love that we are to minister to each other. The church is to be God's agent of healing in the broken world.

A nine-year-old boy fell off his bike, wounded his pride, skinned his knee and elbow and was in tears when he came into the house. Mother immediately sized up the situation and gave him lots of tender loving care as she not only washed his wounds but kissed his "owies." Somehow it was mother's special medicine of "owie kissing" which made the little guy stop crying. Now you and I know there is no medical healing in kissing an "owie." In fact it might even spread germs. But it sure worked wonders on this little boy. Nothing in this world heals like love.

Someone has said, "Show people love—real non-judgmental love—and you have released a powerful, healing force in their lives."

At a recent Pastor's Class, which is our membership class, we asked people, "Why did you come to New Hope and what brought you back?"

One young lady with tears in her eyes, answered, "Seven years ago I came to New Hope but was very mixed up and left and went into a life of sin. For many years I was separated from Christian people, doing my own thing.

"Recently when I got sick of sin, wanting to come back to God, I went to several churches but did not find acceptance in any of them. Then I came back to New Hope, where people had known me before, and they didn't even ask me about all the stuff in my back yard. They didn't even want to know the details of my sin. All they said was they loved me and we'd go from here, with Christ's help, to make something beautiful out of my life. Here at New Hope Community Church I have found healing love for my broken life."

Over the years we have seen thousands of people find healing and wholeness in a loving atmosphere of acceptance and forgiveness. Where Christ is allowed to be glorified and to have His way, there will be *Love, Acceptance and Forgiveness,* as Jerry Cook describes it in his fine book by that title. And where there are these elements, broken people will become whole people. Restoration will be the practice and not the exception.

III. LOVE IS A MOTIVATING FORCE

A close friend said to me the other day, "Dale, you're forty-six years of age and you've worked hard all your life. For the last twelve years you and Margi have given everything that you have to bring New Hope from zero to a church ministering to thousands of people. Why don't you just take it easy, enjoy life?"

I answered my friend, "But, you see, there isn't anything I would rather do than God's work."

I understand Paul's words when he said, *"Love compells us."* The last words of the old hymn, "When I Survey The Wondrous Cross," express what I feel in my heart: "Love so amazing, so divine, demands my soul, my life, my all." Having received all of God's love, how can I do less than serve Him with my best? As for me, so long as I live I will give myself in loving service to God and others.

The Holy Spirit is our motivator. *"And we feel this warm love everywhere within us because God has given us the Holy Spirit to fill our hearts with his love"* (Romans 5:5, LB).

The more we fellowship with the Holy Spirit, the more we will be motivated by His love within us. To want to love God with all our heart and mind and soul, as He commands us, becomes our greatest desire.

Why do you do what you do? What motivates you? Studies of industry have shown that when people are motivated, productivity is increased. These studies also reveal that money by itself does not motivate very many people. Most people need something better to work for. Love is the purest, most positive motivation there is. The Holy Spirit is motivating you right now to relate to people, not out of fear but out of love. Say, "Yes, Lord, yes."

When love is your motivation you don't care so much who gets the credit. Living in love gives you such a sense of rightness and wholeness that you feel good about yourself. You use your spiritual gifts in ministry to others not to show off but because you are motivated by the Holy Spirit.

A wise leader will understand well the love motivation of the Holy Spirit and will cooperate with the Holy Spirit by appealing to his people on that level.

Working with volunteers in a church, it is important to learn that you can't make people do anything. A story I've enjoyed for years concerns a ten-year-old retarded boy who goes shopping with his sister. He bumps up against the shoe rack knocking it over. An irate salesman who has had his fill of Christmas shoppers, grabs the boy, applies pressure and starts yelling at him to pick up every shoe, not noticing that the boy is retarded. The boy shakes his head and yells, "No, no, I'm not going to do it."

The wise older sister sizes up the situation quickly, kneels down and begins to pick up the shoes. As she smiles at him, loving him, he soon begins to respond by helping to pick up the shoes.

When the shoes are all picked up and they rise to leave, the sister looks at the clerk and says, "Mister, you got to love him into doing it."

The way to have more workers in your church than you know what to do with is literally to love them into ministry. Isn't that what Jesus was doing when, on that last night, He washed the disciples' feet? (see John 13)

IV. LOVE IS A UNIFYING FORCE

To be successful in the Christian life and to be successful in ministry as a church, we really do need each other. It was our Lord's last prayer that we might experience oneness (see John 17). Paul taught that the success of the church was dependent upon its unity and that unity would only become a reality where God's kind of love was being put into practice (see Ephesians 4).

Recently a church expert spent a month at our church observing, analyzing, and trying to come up with the secrets of what's making this church successful. One of the principles he cited in his written report was that this church has unity amidst diversity.

What did he mean? He meant that a oneness springing from a deep love for Christ and one another caused us to work together for the good of each and for the accomplishment of the vision God has given to us to reach Portland, Oregon. We are not isolated individuals. Though we are unique persons, we belong on the same team. We help each other to become so much more than any of us can become by ourselves. Because of our love there is synergism, which means there is a miracle of multiplication of abilities as we function together. We are so much more together than the total of our separate parts.

Ephesians is clear that the kind of love that brings unity is a love that overlooks faults and that is led by the Holy Spirit. This love seeks peace one with another. At the same time it respects the uniqueness of each person's calling and spiritual gifts. It helps each person to develop to the fullest in ministry both to the body and outside the church. Love respects each person, honors each, frees each to be himself or herself. Yes, love gives up selfishness for the good of the whole body.

Where there is this unity of love, every person from the custodian to the senior pastor is equally important and called of God to ministry.

With years comes greater wisdom. The older I become the more I realize that in the Christian community we are to live not in competition but in cooperation. When other pastors in my community succeed, I succeed. When they fail, I fail. One of our highest callings may be to help make each other successful.

I heard of a remarkable dream a man once had. People were sitting along both sides of a scrumptious banquet table that was covered with delicious food of every variety. But everyone had a severe handicap. Their arms were stiff and would not bend at the elbow. They could reach the food but were unable to get it into their mouths. What a frustrating experience! With food right in front of them, they were going hungry.

Finally someone got smart and started feeding his neighbor. His neighbor, in return, fed him. Before long all were enjoying the delicious banquet. Wonderful things happen when Christian people learn to feed each other. Galatians 6:2 says it, *"Bear ye one another's burdens, and so fulfill the law of Christ."*

Tradition records that John, the beloved, was the last disciple to die. He lived to be in his nineties and became known as a disciple of great love. But that was not always so. As a young man he was known as "the son of thunder."

On one occasion when a Samaritan village did not welcome Jesus and His disciples, John became so offended at being rejected that he wanted to call fire down from heaven and have them burnt up (see John 9:54). In other words, he had no patience or tolerance with people who didn't treat him as he thought he should be treated.

*LOVE NEVER CONDEMNS BUT ALWAYS SEEKS
TO SAVE AND RESTORE. LOVE DOES NOT DO AWAY
WITH PEOPLE SIMPLY BECAUSE THEY DO NOT*

DO WHAT YOU WANT. LOVE RESPECTS OTHER PEOPLE'S RIGHTS TO DIFFER AND BE DIFFERENT

As an old man, tradition tells us, John spent his last years at Ephesus. On Sundays they would carry him to church and from time to time they would beg him to tell how it was to have been with Jesus. Anxiously they would wait for the famous, beloved disciple to speak the words. John would say, *"Beloved, let us love one another."* When he was asked again and again, he would repeat the same words, *"Little children, love one another."*

V. LOVE IS A FREEING FORCE

Most problems in churches arise for the same reason that relationship problems arise in homes, businesses and every place else in our society. When people feel insecure and relate out of fear instead of love, anything but good happens. I have known pastors with tremedous gifts, men who loved God, but due to an insufficiency of God's love in their daily spiritual diet, they became insecure and started reacting to people instead of responding in love. Let's admit it, when any one of us feels insecure, unsure of our acceptance with our peers, we start reacting in strange ways. Without the security of love there is bondage and warring both within and without.

There can be no real freedom without love. This freedom of love is ours. It's God's gift to us. In I John 3:1 we read these words, *"How great is the love the Father has lavished on us, that we should be called children of God! And that is what we are" (I John 3:1, NIV).*

There is no limit to God's love. It is not held back but lavished upon us. Given to us as we are, where we are. As His children it is our special gift. Receive it, claim it, bask in it, let it sink into your inner being and fill your life with acceptance, forgiveness, love.

One of the greatest things we can do for each other in the Christian community is to affirm God's love to one another by affirming each other in love. The leaders in your church need your affirming love more than anything else.

A church in our community continues to go through staff people one after another. What's wrong? The problem is that as talented as the senior pastor is, he feels insecure. Whenever a staff person begins to excel, he's threatened. But a part of his insecurity is that the people expect too much from him. What a difference it would make if the pastor and people would become secure in God's love.

To be myself frees me as pastor. It frees me to say I have goofed or made a mistake and to ask for forgiveness and to move on in our adventure together. Because love forgives, while resentment, hate and anger bind up. So many good people are enslaved to their own feelings. Their ill feeling binds them to the person that they have bad feelings toward. So many churches are bound up because what they are experiencing and living is not love. **Jesus wants to set us free.**

Say yes to Jesus; let His love flow through your life. Live in the power and the love of the Holy Spirit and be free from fear, free from bondage, free to excel. Be free to relate in love and free to be everything God wants you to be. Oh, the power of liberating love!

VI. LOVE IS A WINNING FORCE

In I Corinthians 13 we read, *"Love never fails."* When you put God's kind of love into practice you will always win. Plant the seeds of love, keep on planting the seeds of love, and you will reap a harvest of love. Be a lover and you will be a winner.

In this world we are in a spiritual battle. Even the creators of Star Wars, the box office movie hit, recognize there is a battle between the forces of good and evil, between the forces of love and hate.

In the most recent segment entitled, "Return of the Jedi," the climax comes in a battle between Luke Skywalker and his father, Darth Vadar, who has been taken over by the dark side. In this battle you see Luke with all the good that is in him, the Jedi, fighting against the forces of hate and evil. The combat on the outside is fierce but inside of Luke is where the real battle is taking place.

There is a fight between good and evil within him. If he allows himself to be taken over by hate in his spirit, then he loses and becomes controlled by the dark side. But here he is, fighting against the force of evil that knows no mercy or justice, but is only determined to conquer and destroy at all costs. You'd better believe that there are destructive forces at work in our world and in our lives. There is a battle raging.

The audiences that have flocked to see "Return of the Jedi" invariably break out cheering when Luke comes out victorious and love wins over hate. In winning over evil, Luke is not only victorious in battle with the sword but he shows love to be the most powerful force. This love breaks the dark spell that's over his father, Darth Vadar, and restores him to the side of good before he departs into eternity. Fortunately the story has a happy ending.

It is no make-believe story that we are in a battle. Either we will be filled with God's Spirit and love or the evil spirit of destruction will take over in our lives. All the resources of God are ours through the Holy Spirit who lives within us. Call upon the name of Jesus. Yield to the leadership of the Holy Spirit. No matter what others do. No matter what attack you're under. No matter how unfairly you've been treated. No matter what's going on in your feelings. Make the love choice because it is the right thing to do.

During a Lay Pastor's training session one of our Lay Pastors who is a nurse gave this testimony. "Today I had an obnoxious patient. I felt like throwing him out the window. But instead, I made the love choice. I rubbed his back and his feet and was kind and considerate toward him. The payoff came toward the end of the day when his entire attitude changed from hostility to friendship." Love won the day. With love you will win, not once, not twice, but again and again.

Love is something you do. And you do it regardless of how you feel. You do it no matter what the other person does or does not do. It is not dependent upon people treating you right. It is dependent upon living in fellowship and in the power of the Holy Spirit. When you have acted in love, you will win even if the other person still misbehaves or rejects you. You will have the feeling of wholeness inside, knowing that you've done what was right in the sight of God. Love always pleases God and love always makes us feel good about ourselves. **Love has a way of breaking through the most impossible barriers.**

Many ministries break down after a couple of years because relationships are not kept up to date. A church leader who really wants to see his church succeed will pay attention to people's wounded spirits and do everything within his or her power to bring

God's healing love into that relationship. Any church leader who keeps on putting love into action will build a winning team. **The church where people learn to keep on loving each other will be a winning church.**

PART II

PRINCIPLES FOR CHURCH GROWTH

PART II - PRINCIPLES

CHAPTER 1 - DYNAMIC
LEADERSHIP PRINCIPLES

Behind every successful organization or enterprise is a leader who knows who he is and what to do at the right time. The late president, Dwight D. Eisenhower, once said, "Leadership is the ability to get a person to do what you want him to do, when you want it done, in a way you want it done, because he wants to do it."

Someone else has said, **"The true leader is not someone who can do the work of ten persons but someone who can organize ten persons to do the work of ten persons."** No leader can be successful unless he can get people to follow him.

PRINCIPLE NO. 1—STRONG LEADERSHIP IS ESSENTIAL
One lesson the church needs to learn is that leadership is a fulltime job. When we look at the successful companies and businesses in America, we discover that they have a board of directors. The board, made up of part time consultants, will meet once, twice, four times a year to act as wise advisors and thinkers. When they meet they talk about major propositions that their leader presents. They are the counselors who evaluate the leader's ideas before he goes ahead and launches them. When they approve the idea, then their leader that they have hired, follows through with making it happen.

In such a case, who is the leader? Leadership does not rest with the board of directors composed of people who meet for a few hours once in a while. The real leadership rests in the hands of the fulltime executive who has been hired by the board to think ahead, present plans, and then carry those plans into action that translates into profit.

In the American church today there has been a vacuum when it comes to having a leader who takes charge. However, all church growth experts agree that the primary catalyst for growth in a local church is having a strong pastor who will be the leader. The pastor must be a man of insight and vision, who is not afraid to make decisions and who, in his walk with God, senses and knows the right time to act.

PRINCIPLE NO. 2—BE A BALANCED LEADER

A task leader is someone who has a clear-cut vision. With a well-defined goal, the task leader advances in singleness of mind. When faced with an obstacle, somehow he or she will find a way to overcome that obstacle. When the goal is the top of the mountain, somehow, someway, the task leader will make it to the top of the mountain. Even if it means leaving half of the flock bruised, battered, and bleeding along the way. The task leader has tunnel vision and can see only the goal. As a result, when people don't do exactly what the leader wants, he or she loses patience with those people and discards them.

What is a cohesive leader? **A cohesive leader is a lover of people.** He will do anything to bring unity, peace and love. He is sensitive to what is going on in other people's lives. He is a shepherd who is straightening out problems and making sure that relationships among his people are well and healthy. He overlooks people's faults and mistakes and just keeps on loving them. He is not going to do anything unless the people are together and united with him.

A church, to be successful, needs both a task leader, like Moses, and a cohesive leader, like Aaron. Without a leader that says, "This is the goal, let's go for it!" churches stay where they are. People have to be challenged and motivated to move from where they are to where God wants them to go. At the same time, a church must have a cohesive leader who loves people and binds them together in a unity of heart and purpose. So much of the strength of a local church is in its oneness and unity.

Which kind of leader are you? In your local church, try to provide both kinds of leadership. Have a strong vision and be sure you transfer that vision to the people you want to go to that peak with you. Be a leader of vision and you will lead your people to new heights. Whatever happens, "Hold fast to dreams, when dreams die, life is a broken winged bird that cannot fly" (Langston Hughes).

PRINCIPLE NO. 3—LEAD WITH LOVE

General Eisenhower once said, "You do not lead by hitting people over the head. Any fool can do that, but it is usually called assault not leadership." In church leadership you must earn the right to lead people by the way you love them. If they know that you love them, really love them, they will follow your leadership.

A leader of visions and dreams must always balance that with love. I understand I Corinthians 14:1 to teach, *"Make love your number one aim."* This means that people are more important than program. When people are hurting, that is what dominates their life. If you don't understand this, you will get upset because people are not doing exactly what you want. All the time, they are bleeding inside. Stop! Find out what is going on in people's lives. Minister to them. In Christ's love make them whole; then they'll be ready to serve the Lord with enthusiasm.

A strong leader must be careful not to run people into the ground with high-powered programs. Loving people is always more important than having your own way.

The best ministry is one that is based on love relationships. Love God first. Build strong, loving relationships within your family. Build loving relationships with your staff members. Build loving relationships with your board members. Build loving relationships with your people. Love the prospects and visitors to your church whether or not they ever do what you wish. The greatest evangelism in this world is just loving people. A successful pastor is one who learns to love people anyway, no matter what they do.

As a leader there are times when you are going to be under attack. People are going to say things about you that are not right or true. You must always resist the urge to fight back. Make the greatest choice of all by choosing to love Christ's way in tough times. Never vindicate yourself. Remember, the Scripture says, *"Do not take revenge, my friends, but leave room for God's wrath for it is written 'It is mine to avenge, I will repay,' says the Lord" (Romans 12:19)*. Trust God with your reputation and with the outcome of your leadership.

Make up your mind that you are going to put Christ's love into practice. You are going to forgive people even before they ask. You are going to eat humble pie if that's what it takes to live at peace and keep harmony in the church. If you'll keep your heart filled with God's love through the power of the Holy Spirit, God will do for you what He did for Joseph of old. He will bring good out of evil, triumph out of tragedy, and victory out of defeat.

PRINCIPLE NO. 4—KNOW WHO YOU ARE

As leader, you must know who you are. Never try to be like someone else or you'll always be second best. God has made you unique. He has given to you special abilities and distinct, marvelous spiritual gifts. Don't get caught in the depressing comparison game. Don't get caught in the self-destructive copycat game but accept who you are. Thank God for the way He has made you, the gifts He has given to you, and develop your leadership potential to the fullest.

Knowing who you are means knowing your strengths as well as your weaknesses. Recognize that no leader has all the gifts and expertise to do what needs to be done by himself. The wise leader is one who enlists the help and services of people who know more than he does in particular areas of ministry. In building a great staff over these years at New Hope Community Church, I have many people working on my staff who excel me personally in particular areas of ministry.

Knowing who you are means also knowing who your church is. What is the calling, the message, the ministry of your church? What is your market? Who are the people you are trying to reach? What are your objectives? What are your beliefs? What are your strengths? What are your weaknesses?

If the leadership of a church does not know who that church is, then the larger it becomes the more pressure there is from new people coming in to push the church all over the map. People who come from other churches already have certain mind sets as to what the church should be.

Every person on a church staff must work within the context of who that church is. Also, every staff person must be loyal to the senior pastor and support his style of ministry. You cannot have people going off in all different directions, doing their own thing , and build a great church.

On one occasion, I had to ask a strong task leader to leave our church because of conflicting style of ministry. I was not comfortable with that style nor were the members of my staff. We have developed over the years a New Hope style of ministry. Men and women on staff understand this and work within that circle. I give them all kinds of freedom, wanting them to be themselves, but at the same time expecting them to be an extension of my style of ministry.

Let me illustrate. New Hope Community Church has always been, what I call, a middle of the road church. By this I mean that we have people who are charismatic and we have people who are not charismatic. The common bonding factor is respect and love for one another. You get someone who is demanding that the church be one way or the other and you cause polarization.

Anyone who insists that the only evidence of being filled with the Holy Spirit is to speak in tongues does not belong on our staff or in our fellowship. On the other hand, if someone insists that people who enjoy prayer language are off base or out to lunch, they won't be comfortable in our fellowship either.

This is an example of what I mean by know who you are. It is very important that a church knows who they are and works to be the best they can of what God has called them to be.

PRINCIPLE NO. 5—SET MEANINGFUL AND MEASURABLE GOALS

Someone has said, "Leadership needs leadership." I have never known a productive leader who did not set definite goals and continually measure his progress toward accomplishment of those goals. Every pastor and every assisting pastor on staff needs to set long range goals, medium range goals, and immediate one-year goals.

At New Hope Community Church our long range goal is to have 100,000 members by the year 2000. We know that this can be accomplished by growing at a rate of 26% a year. Other goals— how many districts, lay pastors and TLC groups to have— are set in accordance with the fulfillment of our long range goal. Already we're thinking about the property and building we will need to facilitate a church of 100,000.

Our medium-range goal is that by 1990 we'll have 15,000 members. We are in the process right now of building a structure that will not only take care of our immediate growth but, by multiplying services, will enable us to reach this medium goal. We have defined exactly how many lay pastors and TLC groups we'll need by 1990 to fulfill this medium-range goal.

When it comes to our one year goal, I go to our four District Pastors and tell them that they can set the goal for membership at whatever they want to as long as it is at least 30% above their present membership. Then the one year goal for membership in each district is broken down into monthly goals. This month-by-month goal chart hangs on the wall of each District Pastor. Each month they measure and monitor how they're doing in reaching their membership goal for that month. Also, in my office on the wall, hangs a monthly charting on how we're doing on our membership goal. With this kind of meaningful, measurable goals, we have been achieving the 26% exponential growth for many years now.

The tragedy of too many churches is that by not setting goals they aim at nothing and succeed at nothing.

Excellence in leadership is the ability to set goals and lead people to accomplishing those goals. As someone has said, "The world stands aside to let pass the leader who knows where he is going." How can you know where you're going unless you set goals?

PRINCIPLE NO. 6—MAKE THE DECISIONS

A leader is one who can make the right decision at the right time. The pastor of a growing church may appear to outsiders to be a dictator. But to the people of the church he is their leader who knows where they're going and is making the decisions to get them there. The leader of a growing church is like the father of a big family making decisions that are best for the entire family.

A leader needs to be in daily fellowship with God in order to be in step with God's perfect timing. A leader must at times be patient and wait for the right hour. At other times he dares not wait but must act quickly. When it comes to things like immorality or threats to the unity of the body, the pastor must not vacillate but act decisively and quickly.

I found that in decision-making it is important to seek counsel of those who know the most about the matter at issue. Where possible, involve them in the decision making process. Also, once a difficult decision has been made, the leader must be able to communicate clearly to his board, pastoral staff, and others the thinking behind the decision. The bottom line is that you cannot be the leader unless you're willing to take responsibility and make decisions at the exact time they need to be made.

In major-league baseball, if a batter gets a hit one out of three times over a period of seasons, he is a shoo-in for the Hall of Fame. No leader is going to make the right decision every time. But the wise leader does everything he can to keep up his batting average. If you've made a bad decision, admit it and get it straightened out as fast as you can.

In the last year-and-a-half I have saved myself from making wrong decisions on a couple of occasions by getting input from my wife and staff members. A wise leader will gather as much information as possible before making the decision. But when it comes right down to it, you are the one who has to make the decision if you're going to lead your church in dynamic growth.

PRINCIPLE NO. 7—SEE AND SOLVE GROWTH-RESTRICTIVE PROBLEMS

A leader is one who spots well ahead of time potential problems and sets out to solve them before they strangle church growth.

Two years ago I spotted a growth restrictive problem we had. Our parking lots were jammed every Sunday. If people cannot find a parking place, you've lost them before they have even gotten into the building. We went to work and built an additional 300-car parking lot. The very Sunday that it was completed we took off on another big growth jump. In the weeks and months that followed we continued our surging growth because the growth-restrictive barrier had been removed.

About a year-and-a-half ago we went into three morning services: at 8 a.m. 9:30, and 11. After almost a year on this schedule, we found that our 8 a.m. service was not doing very well, while the other two services were packed out. What could we do? We had a growth-restrictive problem in that we did not have the best possible times for our three services. We changed the morning schedule so that our three services are now at 9 a.m., 10:30 and 12 noon. The amazing thing is that the 12 noon service has more visitors in it than any of our other services. We discovered that many unchurched people stay up late on Saturday night, sleep in on Sunday morning, and enjoy coming to a noon service. Now instead of two meaningful morning services and a lame one, we have three thriving, growing morning services.

It's up to the leader to spot growth-restrictive problems and give leadership in solving those problems so that growth can continue. One of the things I believe very strongly is that if we will keep the growth-restrictive problems solved, it is natural for a healthy church to grow. Not only is it natural, it is God's will. And, if we keep the growth-restrictive problems solved, it will happen.

PRINCIPLE NO. 8—BE A COMMUNICATOR

A leader must be a successful salesman. He must communicate the truth as he sees it to his people. In getting ready for the building of our 3000-seat sanctuary, here are some of the ways I communicated the need for funds. I began with communicating to our entire staff. In response, all of them made financial commitments out of their hearts to our new building. Next I went to the church board and communicated the need for financial commitment. They, too, responded generously by making faith-sized commitments beyond their tithe for the new project. Then we went to a Rendezvous with Destiny committee made up of many of our top givers. Once they grasped the vision and challenge, they responded with commitments to some very large gifts.

Then we selected and called together our top 400 givers, asking them to serve as a Booster's Club. Almost without exception, each made a financial commitment to our building project. Then, for a four-month period, five mornings a week, I had breakfast with selected members from our congregation at which time I communicated out of my heart about the need for our new building, allowing them to ask any questions and dialogue with me about the project. It was one of the most meaningful times I've ever spent in getting close to a large percentage of our membership. I also gained weight during those four months.

We discovered that some of our people could not come at the early morning hour so we scheduled evening gatherings at which I communicated my heart concern. We talked back and forth about what New Hope meant to us and about our mission to build a new structure to reach more of the unchurched thousands.

Then each Sunday over a period of eight to ten weeks one of our lay couples shared a three-minute testimony about the need for the new building and their commitment to it. Along with this we kept communicating in our weekly publication.

The communication did not stop when the commitments were made. It continues each month through a letter mailed to each person who has made a commitment. In this letter is an update on what's happening in our building project, as well as an accounting of the recipient's giving toward the project.

It has been my experience that whenever communication produces understanding, then you get the positive response from people that you want. It's the things that people don't understand that give you the problems in a church. Every successful leader must be a communicator.

One of the keys to the success of President Reagan has been the fact that he is a tremendous communicator. He is able to sell his ideas to the American people through the way he communicates over television. We probably have never had any president to match President Reagan's ability to communicate. In a growing church the pastor is a good communicator.

PRINCIPLE NO. 9—RELEASE LAY PEOPLE FOR MINISTRY

Recently a woman in her early thirties, a mature Christian, dedicated to the cause of Christ went to her pastor and presented herself for volunteer full-time ministry. The senior pastor did not know what to do with her. After she persisted with her offer over several months, he became somewhat irritated with her and delegated her to one of his assistant pastors.

When she went to the assistant pastor, presenting herself for full-time ministry free, he asked, "What if 50 people came in here, like you, and said they wanted to minister? It would be chaotic. We can't let you run around being a minister. Now we can use you as a secretary."

The woman persisted that she wanted to minister to people. God was calling her to get involved in people's lives: to love them, to pray with them, to win them and disiciple them. Sorry to say, the pastors of this particular church were so interested in protecting their own territory that they had no concept what it means to release lay people for ministry.

Question—What would happen if ten people walked into your church and told your senior pastor that they wanted to present themselves for full-time ministry, free? What would happen?

I believe that there are literally millions of lay people who want to be released for ministry. It's time that, as clergy, we stop protecting our own territory and stifling the work of God and start doing what we are supposed to do—make lay people successful in ministry. This is the teaching of the Word of God (Ephesians 4:12-13).

Pastor, let go! Learn to trust the Holy Spirit not only to protect your office but to minister through called and chosen lay people. Trusting the Holy Spirit is trusting people to minister.

The big question is, who's in charge? You or the Holy Spirit? If you will lose yourself to the control and direction of the Holy Spirit, you will find yourself the pastor of a thriving, successful ministry.

Speaking of protecting your office, it is a proven fact that when people are ministering and using their spiritual gifts, they are fulfilled and satisfied. Satisfied people, instead of being upset with their pastor and sitting around sniping and complaining, are going to be happy workers together with their pastor.

PRINCIPLE NO. 10—USE POSITIVE MOTIVATION

A pastor of a growing church will be a motivator, continually encouraging people in the work of ministry. But how do you do that? I believe very strongly that we should not motivate people out of fear but out of love. Fear can be very effective in getting people to do what you want, but it won't last. It is a proven fact that if people work out of fear, when the boss is away they stop working.

In II Timothy 1:7 we read these words: *"God has not given us the spirit of fear but of power and of love and of a sound mind."* When people are motivated out of love, they serve with positive enthusiasm. They are growing in their own person and ministry, and consequently the whole body is growing strong in love and faith.

There are five positive ways for a Christian leader to motivate others. They are:

> recognition
> praise
> meaningful and measurable goals
> advancement and financial rewards
> love

When people know that you value them and love them, they will do almost anything for you. People will work harder for recognition, praise, and love than they will for a monetary reward.

One thing often lacking in the church is a well-defined progression for people's achievement and advancement. In our New Hope ministry we have three levels of achievement for our lay pastors: Lay Pastor in training, Lay Pastor, and Senior Lay Pastor. Beyond this, on staff, we have Assistant Pastors and District Pastors who almost always have come out of the lay pastor ministry. Any lay person ministering at New Hope knows that the sky is the limit for them when it comes to ministry. The bigger their ministry becomes, the more the Senior Pastor likes it and rewards it. Nothing succeeds like success. Whatever gets rewarded gets done.

As an individual you have only 168 hours in each week and a limited amount of energy. The only way you can extend and expand your time and leadership is to delegate responsibilities and ministries to others. The more people you have helping you, the more work you can accomplish. Also, other people need to be used. There's a well-known principle that either you use them or you lose them. The person who tries to do everything himself loses all the way around.

In delegating to other people, it is important to make sure that the work is something they want to do. They must accept the resonsibility and be challenged by it. Then you need to hold them accountable. For example, I get a written report from each pastor on my staff every Friday morning.

When I read that report, I know what they have done for the week.

Each of our more than 525 Lay Pastors, at our training meetings, turn in a weekly ministry report. We get an additional report of every Tender Loving Care meeting conducted during the week.

If one of our Lay Pastors does not come to the training meeting he is contacted by either the Assistant Pastor or District Pastor over him and held accountable. If this problem of not attending training persists, then he will be disciplined and released from being a Lay Pastor.

PRINCIPLE NO. 12—MAKE OTHER PEOPLE SUCCESSFUL

There's an old saying, **"You can get everything in life you want, if you help other people get what they want."** I confess to you that at this point in my life and ministry I get my greatest satisfaction out of making other people successful. The way to get your church growing by leaps and bounds is to make other people successful. For every person who becomes successful in ministry in your church, you become that much more successful as the leader and pastor. Every time you give it away you end up having more.

It's important as the leader that you get so filled with the Holy Spirit, so secure in God's love, so free in being the person God's called you to be that you can not only release other people for ministry but do everything you can to make them successful. A growing church will have multitudes of people who are serving and being successful in ministry.

PRINCIPLE NO. 13—CULTIVATE AND MAINTAIN GOOD RELATIONSHIPS WITH YOUR PEOPLE

A leader must become a student of human relationships. He must have a sensitivity to the spirit of a person as well as to the spirit of his church. Misunderstandings and ill feelings will do more to stop the flow of power and love and outreach in a church than anything else. The concerned pastor must pay attention to the spirit that exists in relationships.

A leader must do everything he can to bring peace and harmony and good will. Often this means taking the initiative and going to people who are too timid or bound to come to you. It means forgetting sometimes about yourself and trying to find out what's wrong and what's really going on in that person's life.

Most of the time when an individual is upset with the leader or with the church, deeper things are going on in their lives than they are talking about on the surface. You've got to be willing to open yourself up and listen so that you find out what is the problem beneath the surface. Help them get it out. Be an agent of forgiveness and healing and restoration. A leader is one who leads in love and does everything to keep God's healing love flowing in the lives of the people.

PRINCIPLE NO. 14—SERVE THE LORD WITH ENTHUSIASM

There is no calling greater than to be called of God to pastor and lead a church into church growth. A person who has been called of God to do this has a rare privilege and a mighty challenge in life. I've always felt humble when I've thought about God's calling on my life. I thank God for the privilege and excitement of ministering. My heart is filled with gratitude. With gratitude you always gain altitude.

Be a leader who serves the Lord with enthusiasm. Your enthusiasm will be contagious. When you're excited, people around you are going to be excited for Jesus. No one wants to follow a deadbeat. No one wants to invest in a sinking ship. But people will line up to follow a leader, called of God, who knows where he's going, who does everything he can to get people to go with him, and who serves God with enthusiasm (see Romans 12:11).

PART II - PRINCIPLES
CHAPTER 2 - DYNAMIC GROWTH PRINCIPLES

It is God's will and plan for your church to be a growing church. Here are eleven principles to help you produce growth in your local church.

PRINCIPLE NO. 1—PUT PRAYER AT THE HEART OF YOUR PERSONAL LIFE AND CHURCH LIFE

It is utterly impossible for you to expect your church to grow without prayer. Many mistakenly think that somehow if they get the right program then church growth will be automatic. This is a wrong approach. The moving power behind a growing church is fervent prayer.

Early on in the Book of Acts we see that signs and wonders and the church exploding in growth were a result of prayer. The mighty movement of God in a church can never take place without prayer. Therefore, as church leaders we must make prayer a priority in our personal life and model prayer for our congregations.

A characteristic that you will find in every growing church is that prayer has been given a central place in the life of the church. At New Hope Community Church we pray together in staff meetings each week. We pray each week in the Lay Pastor training sessions. We teach our leaders to make prayer an important part of the Tender Loving Care small group meetings that meet throughout our city.

And every morning from 6:30 to 7:30 is Prayer Hour here at

New Hope Community Church. At Prayer Hour we pray prayers of praise, prayers of petitions and intercession, and we pray for the healing of people in their lives. The more we are learning how to pray the more the power of God is being released through our many need-meeting ministries. Where is the prayer center in your church?

PRINCIPLE NO. 2 - LEAD PEOPLE INTO PERSONAL FELLOWSHIP WITH THE HOLY SPIRIT

Without people being filled with the Holy Spirit, fellowshipping with the Holy Spirit and flowing in the Holy Spirit, church growth will not be a reality. The Bible said it in Zechariah 4:6, *"It's not by might, nor by power, but by my spirit, saith the Lord of hosts."* Where the Holy Spirit is given right-of-way and responded to with the words, "Yes, Lord, yes", many of our mistakes and inadequacies will be more than made up for and the work of the Lord will be blessed and multiplied manyfold. Every page of the history of the early church is filled with the person of the Holy Spirit. It was the Holy Spirit acting in and through the actions of the disciples which made the early church experience exponential growth. I've discovered that when I have been fellowshipping with Him, then my ministry is fruitful. Every month there are many new converts in our church because we are cooperating with the Holy Spirit. Through the Holy Spirit salvation flows in the name of Jesus. Through the Holy Spirit healing flows in the name of Jesus. Through the Holy Spirit people are called and motivated into ministry. Through the Holy Spirit those in despair are given new hope. Through the Holy Spirit the broken are being made whole. Through the Holy Spirit those with sorrow find that their night is turned into a new song in the morning.

The leader who wants to pastor a dynamic church will know the Holy Spirit himself and will be leading his people into the Spirit-filled life.

PRINCIPLE NO. 3—MAKE EVERY WORSHIP SERVICE A CELEBRATION

Many churches are so dignified they are dull. The music is listless, the preaching is unexciting. The architecture is without color or imagination. The people attend not with enthusiasm but out of duty.

We live in a day in which people are beaten down emotionally throughout the week. When they come to church they need a positive lift. At New Hope Community Church every service is a celebration to the fact that Jesus Christ is alive.

The music of various kinds is uplifting and really moves people into the presence of Jesus. Even the choir numbers are geared not for performance but for ministry and leading people into the presence of Jesus. An orchestra adds to the celebration and praise.

The preaching is positive and uplifting. People are given hope and faith and love. With these three wonders inside of them they can leave church ready to face anything, knowing that Christ will make them more than overcomers. The sermons are practical and well illustrated so the people can understand them and make application of them in their lives. In every service we make the unsaved people not uncomfortable but thirsty for Jesus.

The whole atmosphere is one of love, acceptance and forgiveness. We find that people will drive many miles to come to a place where they feel not condemned but accepted, loved and forgiven. It's amazing what marvelous changes will take place in people's lives if you will show them the unconditional love that Christ died to provide.

In every service we have a Garden of Prayer time. We invite whoever has a need to come and kneel at the Garden of Prayer. Lay Pastors come and kneel beside them or stand close by, gently placing hands on their shoulders and quietly praying. The love that flows and the power of God present is marvelous. While the pastor prays, the work of God is carried on at the Garden of Prayer and through the congregation as people stand in friendship holding each other's hands.

Every time we worship, the miracles of salvation, healing, renewal, and spiritual growth take place because we come to the celebration expecting to meet together with God. There is a sense of excitement and an atmosphere of love when you walk into one of our New Hope services.

PRINCIPLE NO. 4—CALL PEOPLE TO A DECISION FOR CHRIST AND A COMMITMENT TO YOUR CHURCH

Month after month we see hundreds brought to a personal knowledge of Jesus in New Hope Community Church's ministries. This is not accomplished by a hard sell, dividing the good guys from the bad guys. **It comes out of loving people, flowing in the Holy Spirit, and simply inviting people at the right moment to respond and receive Christ into their lives.**

People come to Christ by standing and praying the sinner's prayer in our worship services, even when the pastor has preached on topics other than salvation. People come to Christ through the personal evangelism of our members. People come to Christ in our pastor's membership classes, in our Tender Loving Care groups, and in our counseling ministries. It's great to see Christ working through our lives to bring others to Himself in so many different ways and places.

I know about a church that multiplied tremendously in the 70's but unfortunately has declined in the 80's. A study of that church reveals that when they were growing they never bothered to get people committed to membership. So, when the tough times came, the people scattered as fast as before they had flocked there.

I believe that people need to make a commitment to a local church body. This is why we have Pastor's Classes twice a month. On the last Sunday of every month we receive new members into our church fellowship at one of the a.m. services. We make a big event out of this.

In faith we speak the words that multitudes of people will join our church each month and it just keeps on happening month after month. More than half the people who attend Pastor's class make first time commitments to become followers of Jesus Christ. To allow people to go on and on without making commitments does neither them nor the church any favors.

PRINCIPLE NO. 5—ORGANIZE YOUR CHURCH WITH THE HOME CELL SYSTEM

For maximum growth, for effective evangelism, for discipling, in order to win people and keep them, commit your church to emphasizing cell groups. At New Hope Community Church we call these our Tender Loving Care groups.

No matter how good your preaching, your music, or anything else at your church, if you do not get people into some small fellowship group you will lose many of them within a two year period. In every major city a large number of people float from one church to another, never really becoming involved as they should.

The greatest system you can have for keeping people is the cell system.

In our church, six to twelve families belong to each Tender Loving Care group. The Tender Loving Care leader is a Lay Pastor who is in training each week, getting directions, and who is supervised on the job by a District Pastor and Assistant Pastor over him or her.

At the weekly training session, each Lay Pastor submits a written report. The Senior Pastor or one of the District Pastors teaches the lesson for the coming week. The Lay Pastors then teach this lesson to their cell groups that meet at whatever time they have chosen to hold it.

In Part Three titled "THE PLAN" we will detail much more information about our Lay Pastors and Tender Loving Care groups. This is God's 20/20 vision and plan for church growth (see Acts 20:20 and Acts 5:42).

PRINCIPLE NO. 6—DEVELOP AND PROMOTE NEED-MEETING MINISTRIES

One of the secrets of success is to **find a need and fill it.** Find a hurt and heal it. The way to establish a need-meeting ministry is to find a big need that many people have. Then find Christians who have the spiritual gifts to minister to that need and who have the vision and heart to see what God can do through such a ministry. These leaders may be staff people or they may be lay members, whichever has the heart and time for the job.

At New Hope Community Church **we have many different need-meeting ministries each of which becomes another point of entry for people into our membership and fellowship.**

Ephesians 4:12 makes it clear that the pastor and pastors on staff are to "prepare God's people for works of service, so the body of Christ may be built up." **Every staff person I have ever hired, I tell them that their job description number one is to recruit, train and motivate lay people to use their God-given spiritual gifts in ministry.** Happy Christians are serving Christians. Our work as leaders is to mobilize our people for ministry.

So in every area of ministry, we have recruiting and training times, and we continue to motivate and encourage the people in their participation in the particular ministry they are serving.

Our Lay Pastor ministry offers three different training sessions every week. We do this so that everyone of our 525 Lay Pastors can get into one of the weekly training sessions. But not only do we have training for Lay Pastors but we have training in every other area of ministry.

Just recently we completed a valuable training tool to be used in our Lay Pastor training sessions titled, "Ministry Skills for Small Group Leaders." This tool consists of 52 individual lessons to assist in equipping and preparing our people for their ministry. Through this tool our Lay Pastors will be provided assistance in helping to develope skills which will not only improve their abilities as leaders but will strengthen all of our small groups. I am convinced that involvement in ministry should take place with training in ministry skills. The two belong together. Whenever one is separated from the other, you do not get the product you need to really be effective in Christ's work.

PRINCIPLE NO. 7—BUILD STAFF OUT OF YOUR OWN LOCAL BODY

As I write this I presently have 30 employees on staff. This includes custodian, secretaries, and ministry staff. Ninety percent of these people have come up out of our own ministry. We are raising up our own staff.

I have yet to experience any major problem with a person on staff who has come up out of our ministry. The few problems that I've had with staff people over the years have always been with people brought in from the outside.

People have come looking for a job or I have gone looking for someone to fill a job. But people who have been hired from within the church do not see themselves as just having a job. They are full participants in the mission and ministry of New Hope. They would do the work of ministry without being paid. I know that because they have done the work of ministry without being paid, before being put on staff. They are teachable, pliable, loyal, and committed to the vision and ministry of New Hope Community Church.

If you are a senior pastor and **you want to build a strong staff that understands your vision and will minister according to your style, then build your staff out of the people who are already being successful in doing the work of minstry in your church.** I believe that it is biblical for people to be faithful in one area of ministry before they are promoted to the next level of ministry. It also offers strong motivation to all of those who volunteer their time in ministry to know that they may have an opportunity to work full-time for the Lord on the church staff.

Talented people in your own ministry will work their hearts out for you on pastoral staff if you will give them the opportunity. Pay them about the same as they were making in secular employment before you challenge them to join you on staff. You'll be surprised at how readily they respond.

PRINCIPLE NO. 8—PURSUE EXCELLENCE IN MINISTRY FROM THE TOP DOWN

Pursuing excellence in ministry by staff develops an air of respect and dignity throughout the congregation. The senior pastor and other staff members set the pace here. Whatever you undertake, do it well and do it first class. If you're preaching sermons, prepare them like a professional. If you're teaching a class, make it the best. If you are administrating business affairs of the church, do so in a first class business manner. The church building does not need to be plush but it should be attractive and well kept. Our purpose is to bring glory to the Lord. We want to give Him our best so that His best can flow through us into the lives of people in our community.

PRINCIPLE NO. 9—BUILD ON YOUR STRENGTHS AND STRENGTHEN YOUR WEAKNESSES

Have the wisdom to know your strengths and, with gratitude to God, build on those strengths. Back on October 14, 1972, when, without any people, my wife, Margi, and I launched the ministry of New Hope Community Church, we used our strengths. Margi was a beautiful singer and I had the ability to preach need-meeting sermons to inspire people. So those are the two things we majored on in the first years of our ministry. Do what you can be successful at and build on the successes.

About two years ago one of the businessmen on my church board asked me this question. **"Pastor, what are the weaknesses of our church?"** I smiled at him and began to tell him about all the marvelous things that we were doing. He pinned me down a little further and said, "I didn't ask you about our successes, but I asked you what are our weaknesses?" Then he went on to explain to me that in his business he didn't make improvements unless he was willing to look at the weaknesses.

That day after he left I wrote down five areas of ministry that I thought showed some weakness.

Amazingly, six months later each of those weaknesses had been turned into a new strength. Have the courage to look at the areas in which your church is weak in ministry and then set out to improve those areas until they become strengths. There is no church in which there is not room for improvement. **Every time we improve something in our church we prepare ourselves to be more effective in ministry for our Lord.**

PRINCIPLE NO. 10—MAXIMIZE YOUR BUILDING WHILE PREPARING FOR THE FUTURE

Prior to the completion of our auditorium we operated a very active and alive church of 4,000 in a building designed for 500-600 people. We did it by multiple Sunday services and multiple ministries every day and night of the week. **The way to make a church grow is to maximize the use of the facilities.**

Most churches make the mistake of constructing buildings too soon. I personally believe that church growth experts have been wrong in suggesting that when the seats are 75% full a church won't grow anymore. What I want to know is, why not? Why can't you have two services instead of one? Why can't you have five or six services on a Sunday? Every time you add another service, you double your capacity and ability to serve people without adding much to your costs. Every time you add a service you increase income and reduce overhead. I don't believe any church is ready to build until it fills its building several times on a Sunday.

That doesn't mean you don't plan the building early. It's important to look ahead and begin planning a building to house the vision that God has placed in your mind and heart. Think about things like accessibility. Give lots of thought to parking. You can't build a great church without surplus parking. The parking lot is just as important if not more important than the kind of building you build. Give a lot of thought and consideration to the sound and to the lighting. It doesn't do any good to build a beautiful building if the people cannot see or hear what's going on in a service. Build your building around the ministries that you have and are going to have. Don't surrender leadership to an architect but tell him what ministries must be facilitated within an inspiring building.

PRINCIPLE NO. 11—BE A PIONEER AND NOT A SETTLER
Settlers play it safe while pioneers reach out to new adventure. Every year you must add something new. If you fail to do this, you're saying to the people, "We have stopped. We are not going to grow any more." A growing church will be a church that is expanding into new ministries.

A church cannot stand still. Either it will be a pioneer and go forward or, if it becomes a settler, it will begin to die. The seeds of decay take root when the church stops advancing. God never meant for us to live as settlers. As the old song put it, "This world is not our home, we're just passing through." God has chosen us and called us to do, *"greater things than these."*

I like these words from an unknown author:

"Grieve not for me, about to start a new adventure. Eager I stand, and ready to depart. Me and my reckless pioneer heart."

PART II - PRINCIPLES

CHAPTER 3 - DYNAMIC CELL GROUP PRINCIPLES

Over many years we have hammered out in the school of application twenty-one principles for successful home cell groups. In our initial training with Lay Pastor recruits we always teach these twenty-one principles. From time to time in the weekly training we reinforce these different principles. It's been our observation over the years that where these principles are practiced the cell group is healthy and thrives. Where these principles are violated the group becomes something less than its best. Over the years whenever we've had a group go sour or get off track, we have discovered that one or many of these principles have been violated.

TWENTY-ONE PRINCIPLES FOR SUCCESSFUL HOME CELL GROUPS

PRINCIPLE NO. 1
THERE ARE THREE ELEMENTS IN AN EFFECTIVE HOME CELL GROUP WHICH MUST BE PUT INTO USE AND KEPT IN EQUAL BALANCE FOR THE BEST RESULTS

A. SHARING —People love to share their lives, one with another. There's nothing like a life-centered testimony to illustrate what is being taught. **The more a person shares with the group**

the more that person feels a part of the group. The other members also feel they know that person better. The goal is to participate in each other's spiritual lives and to become a real family together.

A word of caution. There have been groups in churches that do nothing but share. Although this experience may be very exhilarating for a few weeks, it will eventually deteriorate and get to be old stuff. Then people will grow tired of coming. In a successful group, sharing is an important ingredient but much more than this happens.

B. **CONVERSATIONAL PRAYER** —In our Tender Loving Care groups we teach people to participate in prayer by having a conversation together with God. The leader and other mature Christians keep their prayers simple. New people begin to see that they, too, can pray.

It is far more beneficial for many people to pray together than it is for one person to do all the praying. First we teach people to praise and thank God in short sentence prayers. Then we teach them to share their needs and to respond by praying one for another.

In every home cell group, prayer should be a growing experience together. In praying, people find answers to the needs in their lives. **In praying, people are drawn together spiritually at a deep level.**

C. **APPLICATION OF BIBLE** —The Bible must not only be studied but it must be applied to daily life. Ask practical questions. What promise does God have here for me? What truth is here that God wants me to apply in my life? What principle does God want me to learn in this lesson? Such questions help make application of the Bible lesson to the daily lives of the people present in the cell group. More than just getting Bible knowledge, they learn Bible application to daily life.

Sometimes a group will major on only one of the three above parts. Invariably that group will burn itself out. But where these three elements are kept in equal balance the group will be healthy and will produce healthy well-balanced Christians. In their weekly report sheets, our TLC leaders are required to tell us how much time has been spent in each of these three activities. We monitor this to see that our groups are kept balanced. Now, admittedly, at one meeting the group may spend most of its time in prayer. At another, most of the time may be spent in sharing. Still another occasion may be heavy in Bible learning and application. What we're looking for is that week after week, all three of these elements are prominent in our Tender Loving Care groups.

PRINCIPLE NO. 2
PARTICIPATION IS THE KEY TO SUCCESS

The more an individual participates in a Tender Loving Care group, the more he or she receives from that meeting. As participation goes up, learning increases and enthusiasm builds. We also develop leaders for new studies to come in the days ahead.

GOAL OF LEADER—The goal of the leader in our home cell system is not to be the authority, the teacher, but to be the guide. The leader guides people into participation, prayer, and application of the Word. There are many people who could never be adult teachers. But with some training and supervision they can become excellent leaders in guiding people in home cell groups.

ARRANGEMENT OF PEOPLE—It is amazing what a difference the way people are arranged makes in their participation. For the best participation arrange your people in a circle without any empty chairs. They need to see each other, feel close to one another, and equally participate. You want to make everyone feel a part of this family meeting together.

RULE—DON'T PRESSURE ANYONE TO PRAY, READ OR SPEAK. Make it easy for the timid person to participate, but do not directly ask anyone to pray, read or speak. Some of you may remember from school days how you would fill up with fear when you thought you might be called on to read or recite. Many adults carry the same fears with them today. Recognize that fact and let people volunteer to read the Scripture, to pray, to respond with insights.

The goal is to help each person in your group participate. In order for this to happen, some outspoken people may need to be restrained. Do this by saying, "If you've already read or prayed, maybe you could let others participate before you take another turn." As a leader, keep things so that those who are timid can see that they, too, have something to offer. Make it easy for them to get involved but don't pressure them. Create a comfortable atmosphere in which they feel valued and realize they have something worthwhile to give.

PRINCIPLE NO. 3
BEGIN AND CLOSE WITH CONVERSATIONAL PRAYER

You begin conversational prayer by thanking God for being with you. This brings the group immediately into the presence of God. It also begins to tune everyone to the Lord and what He wants to do in this special time together.

Sometimes people will come with heavy hearts. If you ignore that and proceed with your study, they will get little or nothing from it. A sensitive leader, following the leadership of the Holy Spirit will make it easy for people to share needs. Then, in the opening prayer lead the others in responding to those needs so people will get freed from their burdens before you move on into the study.

We always close our time together with more conversational prayer. This time we respond to the truth that we've learned and make application of it in our lives. Once again we pray for each other's needs, interceding for the requests of individuals and for our church.

PRINCIPLE NO. 4
RESPOND LOVINGLY TO A NEED
EXPRESSED . . . IMMEDIATELY

In James 5:16 we read, *"Admit your faults to one another and pray for each other so that you may be healed" (LB)*. We teach the people in our cell groups three principles from this verse . 1—We are to admit our faults and needs one to another. 2—We are to pray for each other. 3—When we do this we become a healing fellowship to each other. TLC groups are intended to be a healing fellowship. We claim the authority that Jesus gave to us. He said, *"I will give you the keys to the kingdom of heaven; whatever you bind on earth will be bound in heaven, whatever you loose on earth will be loosed in heaven" (Matthew 16:19, NIV)*.

TEACH PEOPLE TO SHARE NEEDS BY EXAMPLE. As Senior Pastor there has been many a time that I've had needs. When I have confessed those needs and asked the people to pray, my own spirit has been touched and healed. The best way to teach people in a cell group to share their needs is for the leader to open up and share areas of his or her own life and ask for prayer.

RESPOND IMMEDIATELY. Through the years we have taught our people that when a request is expressed, the time to respond is immediately. In fact there is something very unloving about allowing a person to hang when they have just shared a deep concern of their life. When you say, "I'll pray for you," it's too easy to walk away and forget it. Love responds not tomorrow but immediately. When we respond immediately with prayers of love and healing, an atmosphere is created in which people can feel free to share their needs, confident that they will be accepted, prayed for, loved.

One technique you might use involves putting a chair in the middle of the circle of your cell group. Sit in the chair yourself and ask members of the group to pray for your needs. When they have finished praying for you, invite anyone else with a need to sit in the chair and be prayed for. Show the people in your group that they can gently lay their hands on the person sitting in the chair and in faith pray for them out of hearts of love. Whenever we have done this we have seen the power of God flow, people's lives changed and transformed, and our Tender Loving Care group bonded together in perfect love.

The rule is this—**needs expressed demand immediate response.** The truth is this—when we respond in prayers of faith we release the healing love of God into one another's lives. The miracle is this—as you pray for someone else your own prayer is answered. **When it comes to healing prayer, we really do need each other!**

PRINCIPLE NO. 5
THE BIBLE IS OUR AUTHORITY AND GUIDEBOOK

In our Tender Loving Care groups we tie our people into the authority of the Word of God. It contains everything necessary for their salvation and Christian walk. It has all the principles and promises that we need to be successful in every area of our lives. From time to time, groups have wanted to study a particular book some author has written. At times, for special reasons, we've allowed them to do that. But over the years we have discovered for the best results the curriculum needs to be the Word of God. It is just what the doctor ordered in people's lives.

PRINCIPLE NO. 6
ENCOURAGE SHARING IN THE GROUP

We want to create an open, friendly atmosphere in which people present can express themselves freely. Each person's opinions and comments must be valued as important. However, if an individual tries to dominate the time and persists in diverging from the subject, the leader will have to insure that attention be centered on the particular verse or passage being studied.

Dialogue is what you're after. People need to discuss the truth of God, sharing with each other and making application of that truth in daily life. Even while you're studying the Word of God, if someone expresses a need, stop right there and respond by praying for the need. If they are encountering difficulties and need counsel or encouragement, ask questions and help them at their point of need. However, a group is not a therapy session. The leader is not a psychologist. People that have deep emotional problems are not to be dealt with in the group but referred to the pastor or to competent counsel.

PRINCIPLE NO. 7
DON'T ALLOW DOCTRINAL DISCUSSION THAT
IS DIVISIVE OR ARGUMENTATIVE

Two things will polarize a group right down the middle: doctrinal disputes and political debates. Don't allow either one to take place in a group. One time during elections this happened in a group that I was in and it created two sides instead of one group. I learned my lesson right then never to allow a group to talk about political candidates in one of our cell meetings.

If someone brings up a doctrinal issue of the kind that divides people, then simply, as leader, make the statement that we do not dispute doctrine here at this meeting. Tell the person you will be glad to talk privately afterward. There are people who at times will use doctrinal differences to divert attention from what really needs to happen in their own lives.

PRINCIPLE NO. 8
PRACTICE MUTUAL EDIFICATION

A **Tender Loving Care group in our fellowship is to be a mutual admiration society.** We are a team together helping each other be everything we can be for God. We want to help build healthy self-esteem in one another. This is a part of loving each other God's way. The principle we practice is the principle of edification—to encourage and build up each other. The leader can best teach this by example. Express words of appreciation. Tell people how wonderful they are and why they are so special. To edify is to build up. In Romans 14:19 we read these words: *"Let us therefore make every effort to do what leads to peace and to mutual edification" (NIV).*

PRINCIPLE NO. 9
LEAD IN LOVE

Our greatest need is to be loved and give love. **Make your home cell group a loving family.** Give each other lots of good Christian love. In our Tender Loving Care groups, when we pray we hold hands in friendship. This brings us together in love. People are encouraged to express their love for one another. It's not unusual in our Tender Loving Care groups to see people giving each other hugs. **Love, acceptance and forgiveness are practiced continually in our home cell groups.**

PRINCIPLE NO. 10
"FOLLOW-UP" ON MEMBERS BETWEEN MEETINGS IS ESSENTIAL

For a Tender Loving Care group to be successful there must be contact between meetings. Those that have not been present must be called on the phone and encouraged and given love. New people should be called in friendship and invited to come and participate and enjoy what's going on. In our Lay Pastor training we help our leaders to overcome their fears of the phone and to make the calls. We also help them learn what to say. We teach them that **phoning people is just loving people.**

PRINCIPLE NO. 11
NEW MEMBERS BEING BROUGHT INTO THE GROUP
WILL KEEP IT ALIVE AND GROWING

Home cell groups that stop bringing new people in become ingrown. After they have been together for five or six months they become very comfortable with one another. That is both an advantage and a disadvantage. It's an advantage in that you want people to have this close Christian heart-to-heart fellowship. It can be a disadvantage if they get so comfortable that they don't want to bring in anyone new.

Every time a new person is brought into the group it gives it a whole brand new life. The way to keep from becoming stagnant is to keep adding new members to the group.

PRINCIPLE NO. 12
HANDLE PROBLEM PEOPLE AWAY FROM THE GROUP
ON A ONE-TO-ONE BASIS

There are in our world not only a lot of troubled people but some very disturbed ones. **You cannot allow a disturbed person to become the center of attention in your group.** If you do this you will ruin your group. Someone who is disturbed, easily misunderstood, or who has to have all the attention should be taken aside by the leader and talked to on a one-to-one basis. Make it clear that you love him or her, that you are glad to talk one-on-one, but that continually rehashing problems or using the group as a dumping ground cannot be permitted. If a leader does not take action and handle this particular problem, he will see his group dissipate.

It is important to have pastoral supervision of cell groups. One of the reasons is that Lay Pastors leading TLC groups are not equipped to deal with getting troubled people out of their groups.

In three or four weeks the group will be ruined if something is not done. A pastor in charge can move in and give the support and strength needed to deal with the troubled person and save the group. No concerned, loving shepherd will allow harm to come to the sheep. Many times one must do what is best for the whole group. **You cannot afford to allow one troubled person to wipe out a whole cell group.**

PRINCIPLE NO. 13
DON'T ALLOW PEOPLE TO CONFESS ANYONE'S FAULTS BUT THEIR OWN

Tony and Martha, although they had been married for 26 years, had not yet learned to live together in harmony. In front of a group Martha seized the opportunity to apply the Scripture lesson to Tony's life and to confess that he had a roving eye. Tony didn't say anything but you could see the anger swelling up inside of him. To be injured by anyone is bad enough. But to be injured by your own mate in front of people you want to think well of you is to multiply that injury many times. Needless to say the husband never came back to the group. For years afterwards Martha kept asking why she couldn't get her husband interested in spiritual things.

Never allow anyone to get by with confessing another person's sin in front of the group. If this happens the leader must immediately take hold of the situation and in good humor remind the group that we have this little rule: we don't confess anyone's faults but our own. (see James 5:16)

PRINCIPLE NO. 14
DON'T ALLOW ANYONE TO DO ALL THE TALKING

If you have one person who has to do all the talking you must politely but firmly intervene. You can do this by saying, "Thank you for your comment. Now let's hear what some others have to say." If the problem persists, take the person aside and explain the need to limit each person's talking so that everyone will have opportunity to participate.

Often gabby people do not realize what they're doing. With a little teaching and guidance they will come into line.

Preachers often do not make good leaders or participants in home cell groups. The reason is that they sometimes do all the talking and become a hindrance instead of a help in the group participation process. The truth of the matter is that we who are preachers and teachers really need to listen to the feedback of other people.

PRINCIPLE NO. 15
BE TUNED UP SPIRITUALLY YOURSELF

The Holy Spirit will be hindered if the leader is spiritually indifferent or troubled with unconfessed sin. A person not free to the working of the Holy Spirit in his own life can hardly be a channel for His working in the cell group. Before every meeting it is essential that the leader spend time alone in fellowship with the Holy Spirit so that he can be a channel through which the Spirit flows and does His work in the cell meeting.

PRINCIPLE NO. 16
KEEP LEARNING, DON'T HAVE ALL THE ANSWERS

To be a successful leader or guide of a small group, a person does not have to be a seminary graduate, or even have attended Bible school for a year. One does not have to know all the answers. But one does have to be a learner. We find that **the best teachers are all learners.** The attitude we want in a home cell leader is: "I don't know all the answers but I am learning how to live God's way. **And here at our TLC group we are learning together."** A good way to handle a question is to ask other people in the group if they know the answer. If no one knows the answer, have everyone study the question for the week and bring back an answer next time.

PRINCIPLE NO. 17
HANG LOOSE AND MAINTAIN A RELAXED SPIRIT
IN THE GROUP

A good leader is one with the honesty and openness that is not afraid to discuss or consider other points of view. Trust the Holy Spirit to be the teacher. Do not feel like you have to have all the answers. After all, you are a guide in leading people into truth, not the expert or big authority.

It's a tremendous asset when a leader accepts himself as a person of worth and then can reach out to other people and make them feel comfortable in who they are. Let God do the changing rather than feeling like you have to change every person to conform to what you think he or she should be.

A good leader learns to be shock proof. Not judgmental or harsh or opinionated, not overly reactive when an individual says something that goes against the grain. If you're really going to let God use your life to reach unchurched people, then you're going to have to be willing to listen to a lot of things that you don't agree with. Give God the opportunity to work and bring that person to Himself as well as to bring them to Christian maturity.

A good leader is not dogmatic or having to force his own ideas or opinions. He believes in the Word of God and the power of the Holy Spirit to work in the person's life.

We really can trust the Holy Spirit. If we create the loving atmosphere, He will do His work.

PRINCIPLE NO. 18
A GOOD SENSE OF HUMOR IS A VALUABLE ASSET

In the Holy Scripture we read, *"A cheerful heart is good medicine, but a crushed spirit dries up the bones" (Proverbs 17:22, NIV).*

We live in a time when people are heavily stressed. One thing they need to find at the home cell meeting is relaxation. Good clean humor and laughing together is marvelous for people who attend the meeting. Recently in a training session one of our District Pastors, Betty Jacques, was speaking on humor from Proverbs 17:22. Pastor Jacques pointed out that laughing does these five things for us:

1) releases tension
2) relaxes our bodies
3) rests our spirits
4) renews our hearts
5) reorients us to see life in perspective

PRINCIPLE NO. 19
WHEN YOU HAVE A NEED IN YOUR OWN LIFE,
ASK YOUR TLC GROUP FOR HELP

Christians are not perfect but they are forgiven. A leader will have needs in his or her life just like anyone else. **You lead and teach other people to deal with their problems by the way you deal with your own.** If you are going through tough spots, confess your need in your group meeting and solicit the prayers and help of your fellow Christians. You never outgrow your need for the help of other Christians. The best leaders are those who keep admitting that they need others.

PRINCIPLE NO. 20
WHEN YOU HAVE A PROBLEM OR NEED HELP,
QUICKLY GO TO YOUR PASTOR OR LEADER
AND ASK FOR IT

One of the great successes of the New Hope home cell system is that our leaders know they can go to their supervisors and find a listening ear and an understanding heart. The supervisor is a fellow Christian who loves them and will pray for them in their time of need. At New Hope Community Church we accept each other where we are and work hard in helping each other be over-comers, successful in life and ministry.

PRINCIPLE NO. 21
REMEMBER … IT'S CHRIST WHO DOES THE LEADING,
NOT US

A good leader is a good follower of Christ—no more, no less. As long as you keep supplying the person and then saying "Yes, Lord; yes, Lord," God will use you to do *"greater things than these."*

PART III

PLAN FOR CHURCH GROWTH

PART III - PLAN

CHAPTER 1 - OUR MASTER PLAN AND ORGANIZATION FOR UNLIMITED GROWTH

Our master plan for church growth on the exponential curve is not something new. It is not the brainchild of this author. Rather, it is the blueprint given to us in Scripture and practiced with overwhelming success in the early church.

20/20 VISION

Here is God's own **master plan** for church growth in your church: *"You know that I have not hesitated to preach anything that would be helpful to you but have taught you publicly and from house to house" (Acts 20:20, NIV).*

In our Lord's own ministry the home was a focal point of heart-to-heart fellowship. He is frequently recorded as having gone into homes, healing someone (see Matthew 8:14-15; 9:23-25; Mark 1:29-31; Luke 8:51-56). Jesus also went into the homes of sinners to draw them into fellowship (see Matthew 9:10-13; Mark 2:15-17; Luke 5:29-32).

The focus on the home as a place of deep fellowship and ministry is also seen clearly in the history of the early church as recorded in the Book of Acts. In some of the very first words about the early church we read, *"All the believers were together and had everything in common. Selling their possessions and goods, they gave*

*to anyone as he had need. Every day they continued to meet to-
gether in the temple courts. They broke bread in their homes and
ate together with glad and sincere hearts, praising God and enjoying the favor of all the people. And the Lord added to their number
daily those who were being saved" (Acts 2:44-47, NIV).* In the
New Testament the Greek word for house, *oikia,* appears at least
ninety times, with nine different references to believers worship-
ping, fellowshipping, or being taught in a house (see Acts 2:2-4;
2:46; 5:52; 10:24-48; 16:25-34; 16:40; 20:17-20; 21:8-14; 28:30-
31).

**The way to build a great church is to follow the master plan
that was so effective in the early church.** Meet in the house of
God on Sunday to celebrate all together the resurrection power of
Jesus. Then, throughout the week, meet house-to-house in small
groups for heart-to-heart fellowship. This New Testament blueprint for building a successful church is in perfect step with meeting the needs of people who are lonely and isolated in this 20th
century. This plan is absolutely perfect for this generation.

At New Hope Community church, in our Sunday services, we
have a celebration with positive preaching, inspiring music, healing,
uplifting prayers and friendly, happy people. Added to this we have
more than 500 Tender Loving Care groups meeting during the week
throughout the metroplitan area where "heart-to-heart fellowship"
takes place. From our own sucess we believe this is the missing link
that churches today need to unleash the mighty signs and wonders
and experience growth by groups.

**If you want to be a pastor of people who are filled with en-
thusiasm and turned on for God, follow this 20/20 vision plan.**
If you want to see the unchurched and unconverted brought to
Jesus, follow this 20/20 Vision plan. If you want to see baby
Christians become strong in the Lord, follow this 20/20 Vision
plan. If you want to develop strong Christian leaders, put this
20/20 Vision plan into action in your church.

PRESENT ORGANIZATIONAL STRUCTURE

Making use of the Post Office's Zip Code map, we have divided
the Portland metropolitan area into four districts. Each of these dis-

tricts is headed by a District Pastor. The District Pastor is over all the members and prospects living in that district.

We have begun to develop our middle management—Assistant Pastors who work and assist the District Pastors in doing their work. Presently we have one Assistant Pastor under each District Pastor. Each district has from 50-60 Tender Loving Care groups that are supervised by the District Pastor and Assistant pastor together. With every 50 TLC groups added in a district, it is our plan to add an additional Assistant Pastor for supervision.

FUTURE ORGANIZATIONAL PLAN

Our goal--to have 100,000 members in the future.

Our goal--to have 10 districts lead by 10 District Pastors.

Our goal--each district will have 12 Assistant Pastors
who will be under a district Pastor.

Our goal--each of the 120 Assistant Pastors will be
responsible for supervising 50-60 TLC groups.

Our goal--this will give us 6,000 Tender Loving Care groups
with 8-10 families per group--a total of 100,000
members being cared for and ministering to each
other on a daily basis.

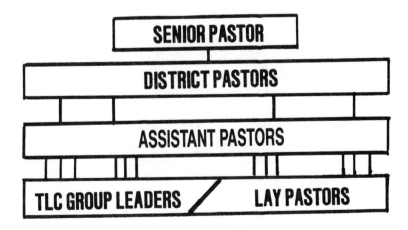

SENIOR PASTOR: The Senior Pastor is over the entire home cell system. He is continually giving the vision and motivating the District Pastors, Sectional Pastors, and Lay Pastors in ministry. Through sermons and communications he is actively recruiting lay people into ministry. He sees that they are given the proper training and supervision to be successful. **The Senior Pastor's heart must be in the home cell ministry if it is to be effective. This is one ministry that cannot be handed over to someone else and forgotten.**

DISTRICT PASTOR: Both Geographic and Specialty District Pastors are expected to have the following leadership qualities: (1) recruit and train others to be effective in ministry; (2) evangelism; (3) vision; (4) lover of people; (5) faith; (6) organization/administration; (7) compassion; (8) enthusiasm.

Specific responsibilities will include: Be accountable to the Senior Pastor for the total ministry of the district; manage the people and the assets of the district; initiate effective evangelism in the district; organize the discipling of every member in the district; set membership goals for the district; supervise all the Lay Pastors and TLC groups in order to make them successful; recruit new Lay Pastor trainees; strive to get every member and prospect into a TLC group; create new groups with new leaders continually; invest one-to-one time with leaders who will help the district grow.

ASSISTANT PASTOR: This person is appointed by the pastoral staff and may be either salaried or volunteer to assist the District Pastor in carrying out the responsibilities of the district.

TLC GROUP LEADER/LAY PASTOR: On this level, lay leadership begins. Lay Pastors are chosen upon completion of the training weekend and three months of a visible life of faith. This is reflected in such areas as: consistent attendance in church and TLC meetings, faithfulness in tithing, enthusiasm and wisdom in the Christian walk, having received the fullness of the Holy Spirit. A TLC group leader is responsible for: (1) the members of his/her TLC group; (2) attendance at a weekly training meeting; (3) leading the weekly TLC group Bible study; (4) being instrumental in evangelism; (5) weekly written reports of personal ministry and the TLC meeting; (6) faithful attendance at the worship services of the church.

Every Tender Loving Care group leader in our system must be a Lay Pastor.

SPECIALTY DISTRICTS

Since the first publication of "20/20 Vision" along with the development of Geographic Districts we have been developing what we call Specialty Districts. A Specialty District is a gathering of people around a common denominator. They have their own District Pastor, Lay Pastors and Tender Loving Care groups. They function much like a geographic district but are not bound by geographic boundaries.

The eight Speciality Districts that we now have operating are as follows:

> Positive Singles' District
> New Life Victorious District
> Youth District
> Children's District
> Women's District
> Music District
> Helps' District
> Young Adult District

PART III - PLAN

CHAPTER 2 - WHAT IS A LAY PASTOR AND WHAT DOES A LAY PASTOR DO?

WHAT IS A LAY PASTOR?

A Lay Pastor is a person who has answered the call from God to do the work of ministry. When it comes to ministering to people at New Hope Community Church, our 450 Lay Pastors are given permission to do all the same things that our staff pastors get paid to do, with a few exceptions. Our paid staff do the preaching and administer the sacraments. Beyond that, our Lay Pastors do all the same things that our paid pastors do in keeping with the amount of time they have to give to ministry.

Some Lay Pastors because of their financial independence, are able to give full time in ministry. Others, who must work at secular jobs to support their families, can give only two to four hours a week. We adjust the Lay Pastor ministry so that it will fit the amount of time a Lay Pastor has to minister, recognizing that people must support their families, not only physically but emotionally and spiritually. There is no way that we could afford to hire people for the thousands of hours of ministry carried on weekly by our dedicated, trained Lay Pastors, Consistently our Lay Pastors average more than 14,000 contacts weekly in one-on-one ministries.

In our home cell system the Lay Pastor's ministry surrounds and comes out of the Tender Loving Care group that he either leads or is the assistant leader.

We believe at New Hope Community Church that **God uses women just like He does men.** An equal number of men and women are Lay Pastors. As Senior Pastor I believe that a woman can do anything that man gives her authority to do. I give the women at New Hope Community Church the authority to carry on the exciting work of ministry. They serve the Lord with great enthusiasm and effectiveness. In this we are careful though that a married woman does not become a Lay Pastor without the permission and blessing of her husband.

FOUR-FOLD WORK OF LAY PASTORS

1. MISSIONARY
"Then Jesus came to them and said, 'All authority in heaven and on earth has been given to me. Therefore go and make disciples of all nations, baptizing them in the name of the Father and of the Son and of the Holy Spirit, and teaching them to obey everything I have commanded you. And surely I will be with you always, to the very end of the age' " (Matthew 28:18-20, NIV).

2. AMBASSADOR FOR CHRIST
"that God was reconciling the world to himself in Christ, not counting men's sins against them. And he has committed to us the message of reconciliation. We are therefore Christ's ambassadors, as though God were making his appeal through us. We implore you on Christ's behalf: Be reconciled to God" (II Corinthians 5:19-20, NIV).

3. SHEPHERD
"When they had finished eating, Jesus said to Simon Peter, 'Simon son of John, do you truly love me more than these?' 'Yes, Lord,' he said, 'you know that I love you.' Jesus said, 'Feed my lambs.' Again Jesus said, 'Simon son of John, do you truly love me?' He answered, 'Yes, Lord, you know that I love you.' Jesus said, 'Take care of my sheep.' The third time he said to him, 'Simon son of John, do you love me?' Peter was hurt because Jesus asked him the third time, 'Do you love me?' He said, 'Lord, you know all things; you know that I love you.' Jesus said, 'Feed my sheep' " (John 21:15-17, NIV).

4. SERVANT

"Therefore, I urge you, brothers, in view of God's mercy, to offer your bodies as living sacrifices, holy and pleasing to God— which is your spiritual worship" (Romans 12:1, NIV).

"...just as the Son of Man did not come to be served, but to serve, and to give his life as a ransom for many" (Matthew 20:28, NIV).

What special joy comes from serving!

THREE LEVELS OF LAY PASTORS

There are three levels of Lay Pastor ministry at New Hope Community Church. **The first level is what we call a trainee.** This is where everyone begins. For the first 90 days each one enters the Lay Pastor ministry as a Lay Pastor trainee.

During this time, trainees are expected to attend the weekly training meeting for continuing supervision and training. They are expected to begin to take an active part in the ministry, beginning where they are and moving to where they want to go.

During this time, they are closely supervised by the District Pastor and Assistant Pastor. At the end of the three month period, if the person in training has proven to be faithful in ministry, then he or she is awarded in a public ceremony the Lay Pastor badge. These badges are worn with great pride and a sense of responsibility to carry out the work of a Lay Pastor.

The second level of our Lay Pastor ministry is the Lay Pastor. The Lay Pastor really becomes the arms and legs of Jesus Christ in our church extended, reaching out, touching people within the body and beyond, taking them into the very presence of Jesus. Continually we admonish our Lay Pastors to be those who bring other people into the very presence of Jesus.

Our third and highest level of Lay Pastor ministry is the earned and awarded position of Senior Lay Pastor. This is a person who has proven faithful and who has walked with the Lord in ministry over a two year period. Their life has, in turn, reproduced the fruits of additional Lay Pastors and other Tender Loving Care groups. The position of Senior Lay Pastor is a very special level of ministry. Several times a year at major events we make

Senior Lay Pastor awards. It is an electrifying moment of achievement and advancement.

Repeatedly we admonish Lay Pastors to work toward becoming Senior Lay Pastors. We motivate on the point that Senior Lay Pastors are those who become grandparents and great grandparents by producing new Lay Pastors and new TLC groups. Some of our Senior Lay Pastors have the joy of having reproduced more than a dozen Lay Pastors and a dozen Tender Loving Care groups. This is how we multiply with growth by groups.

WHAT IS EXPECTED AND REQUIRED OF A LAY PASTOR?

We require the same things that Timothy outlines as qualifications for deacon in the Scriptures, I Timothy 1:3-13 specifically. In our fellowship, we expect Lay Pastors:

1) To be consistent and committed in living the Christian lifestyle. With a daily commitment to prayer as a top priority.

2) To see the vision of New Hope Community Church and be loyal to its leadership, and committed to accomplishing the great things that God has called us to do.

3) To be dependable and accountable to those placed in leadership.

4) To be led and controlled by the Holy Spirit.

5) To be a regular participant in a TLC group, either by leading a group, or by assisting in the leadership of that group.

6) To attend a weekly Lay Pastor's meeting—on Wednesday (9:30 to 10:30 a.m. or 5:30 to 6:30 p.m.) or Sunday (5:15 to 6:15 p.m.).

7) To wear the Lay Pastor's badge each Sunday. Be sensitive to people's needs and respond to those needs.

8) To come to the Garden of Prayer during Sunday services and pray for those who have come forward.

9) To work faithfully and diligently each week in doing what God has called us to do.

10) To be a member of New Hope Community Church, complete the special Lay Pastor training and pass a written exam, and be selected by the pastoral staff.

11) To be faithful in tithing and giving time.

12) To maintain a solid family life.

STEPS TO ADVANCE AS A LAY PASTOR

One of the weaknesses of most churches is that there is no opportunity for lay people to advance in ministry. **God has created us with a need to reach for new levels of attainment. Realizing this, we have built into our Lay Pastor program the opportunity for advancement and achievement.** Above the Senior Lay Pastor level is the opportunity to become an Assistant Pastor. Above that is the level to become even a District Pastor. We believe very strongly that people are to begin ministering where they are. If they are faithful, God will increase and multiply their ministry.

LEVEL I - TRAINEE....

1) Committed to Christ and wanting Him to be NUMBER ONE in your life.

2) A member of New Hope Community Church

3) Take Lay Pastor training.

4) Pass Lay Pastor examination.

5) Accept an assignment, as either the leader or the assistant leader of a TLC group.

6) Approved by pastoral staff.

7) Attend the weekly Lay Pastor's training meeting.

8) Give a written report each week for personal ministry.

LEVEL II - LAY PASTOR....

1) Serve as a Lay Pastor trainee for at least three months.

2) Accept an assignment as either the leader or the assistant leader of a TLC group.

3) Attend the weekly Lay Pastor's training meeting.

4) Give a written report each week for personal ministry.

5) Be faithful in attendance at the worship services of the church.

6) Be faithful in tithing to the Lord's work.

LEVEL III - SENIOR LAY PASTOR....

1) At least two years of continuous faithful service.

2) Faithful attendance in all of the Lay Pastor events.

3) Follow-up on Friendship Cards that are assigned.

4) Successful leadership in Tender Loving Care groups.

5) Reproduce themselves in the lives of other people, specifically other Tender Loving Care group leaders and new Lay Pastors having come from their ministry.

6) Periodically visiting other TLC groups to instruct and encourage them.

7) Impeccable moral lives...biblically grounded.

8) History of humility and faithfulness to Jesus, church and pastoral staff.

9) Consistent tithing record.

10) Solid family life—this applies to a single family as well as a married family.

TRAINING OF A LAY PASTOR

1. Three times a year, on the first weekends in October, February, and May, we have what we call our Lay Pastor Super Bowl. For six weeks beforehand through sermons and church communications, we recruit people to come to the Lay Pastor Super Bowl to become Lay Pastor trainees. On the first night we invite all of the Lay Pastors to come in to help get the new trainees off to a good start as well as rejuvenate and make successful the present group of Lay Pastors.

By the time Saturday afternoon comes we have laid down all the qualifications and basic training for being a Lay Pastor.

The weekend is concluded by having everyone who wants to become a Lay Pastor in training to sign a Lay Pastor Commitment Sheet.

2. MEET ONE-ON-ONE WITH DISTRICT PASTOR AND ASSISTANT PASTOR. Within the week following the Super Bowl weekend training, every new recruit meets one-on-one with the District Pastor and the Assistant Pastor of the district in which he or she will work to spell out exactly how the new Lay Pastor will begin ministry. At this point we leave nothing to chance. If a person is going to be a Lay Pastor in training, he or she must become involved in ministry. We do not allow any free rides.

3. WEEKLY LAY PASTOR TRAINING—Every Lay Pastor, from all three levels, is expected to be at one of the three weekly training sessions we hold. At this training session, each one is to turn in Lay Pastor Weekly Report Sheet.

At the training meeting we worship in songs of praise, we pray, we share victories. There is motivation, teaching about ministry, and about principles of being a successful Lay Pastor and Tender Loving Care group leader. The printed lesson is taught for the coming week.

Most of the time the Senior Pastor writes these lessons. Often he ties them into a series that he is preaching on Sunday morning or an emphasis that he thinks the entire church needs at that time. When he's out of town, one of the District Pastors writes the lesson and teaches it.

When the Lay Pastors enter a training meeting, one of the first things they see is their own district table. They place their reports in the box on the table and pick up new report sheets for the coming week. They pick up their lessons for the week. Also there is an envelope that has within it assignments to new people, new members, prayer requests, new converts, TLC prospects, and all the other work of ministry that needs to be done with people. The Lay Pastor takes the assignment, carries it out and then returns it, with a report, to the box on the table the following week.

At New Hope Community Church in each service we ask everyone present to fill out a Communication Card. This information goes Monday morning to our Information Center where the necessary data is taken from it. Then by noon it goes to each of our four district secretaries who, in consultation with their District Pastors, prepare the assignments for the Lay Pastors for the week.

ACCOUNTABILITY AND DISCIPLINE

For a Lay Pastor ministry to be effective on an on-going basis, **people must be held accountable for what they have committed themselves to do.** This is where supervision becomes so important. For example, if a Lay Pastor repeatedly misses the training meeting, the District Pastor will call him to account. If report sheets are not filled out and brought in, the Lay Pastor is asked why. From time to time we have found that we have to, in love and firmness, discipline Lay Pastors. Discipline is always for the good of the person as well as the health of the body. Here are some statements about discipline that are in our training manual and are carried out in our ministry.

DISCIPLINE FOR MORE EFFECTIVE MINISTRY

1. Each person who is in the Lay Pastor ministry will be accountable to:

    a. Senior Pastor, Dale Galloway

    b. Immediately accountable to their District Pastor.

2. A person in the Lay Pastor ministry may be disciplined for any of the following reasons.

    a. Not carrying out the ministry assignment that was accepted.

    b. Not attending the weekly training meeting.

    c. Any kind of immorality.

    d. Any spirit of bitterness, disloyalty, or strife which causes harm to other people around them in the church.

    e. False doctrines being taught.

PROCEDURE FOR DISCIPLINE

1. The discipline will vary from a loving and prayerful talk with the District Pastor to the point of asking the person to step out of the Lay Pastor program for a given period of time which is in line with the offense.

2. If the District Pastor requests it, then the Lay Pastor badge will be surrendered.

3. **All discipline will have as its goal the redemption and restoration of the individual as well as the good of the Body of Christ.**

PART III - PLAN

CHAPTER 3 - WHAT ARE TENDER LOVING CARE GROUPS ANYWAY?

During his illustrious career, Babe Ruth, the king of baseball, hit 714 homeruns. Babe Ruth is not only an American hero but a legend among sports fans.

But in Ruth's long baseball career he was not always king of the mountain. In one of his last full major league games he played terribly. It was the Braves versus the Reds in Cincinnati. Age had caught up with the Babe and he was no longer agile. During the game he fumbled the ball and threw badly. In one inning alone his errors were responsible for most of the five runs scored by Cincinnati.

As Babe walked off the field after that game and headed for the dugout, the booing of the fans reached his ears and cut to the quick of his heart.

At that moment a young boy who idolized the hero jumped over the railing and into the playing field. With tears streaming down his face, he threw his arms around the legs of Babe Ruth.

The baseball great didn't hesitate for one second. He picked up the boy, hugged him, and set him down on his feet, patting his head gently.

The noise from the stands came to an abrupt halt. Suddenly there was no more booing. A hush fell over the entire ball park. In those brief moments, the fans saw two heroes: Babe Ruth, who in spite of a dismal day on the field could still care about a little boy; and a small lad, who cared about the feelings of another human being. Together they had melted the hearts of a hostile crowd.

What is a home cell group? At New Hope Community Church we call it our Tender Loving Care group. It's where people gather in Christ's name and really care for one another. It's belonging and being loved by others. It's being accepted where you are and giving acceptance to other people who come into the circle. It is where heart-to-heart fellowship takes place. It is where the circle of love is continually being enlarged to take in one more person.

In one of our recent staff meetings, our District 2 Pastor, Jerry Schmidt defined a Tender Loving Care group as "wherever New Hope people circle and pray." When he said this we all had a good laugh but then realized that this definition really hit the nail on the head.

WHY DOES A CHURCH NEED HOME CELL GROUPS?

EVERY CHURCH SHOULD HAVE HOME CELL GROUPS BECAUSE THAT IS THE 20/20 VISION GIVEN TO US IN ACTS 20:20. To hold services on Sunday and not meet during the week in homes and other places is to be only half a church. Home cell groups are not something we can just take or leave like another program, but it is God's plan for the building of His church on this earth.

WITH THE HOME CELL MINISTRY THERE IS NO LIMIT TO HOW LARGE A CHURCH CAN BECOME. The establishment, growth and multiplication of groups in a church means that the barriers are broken. Those things restricting growth are done away. There are no more limits and restrictions placed on lay people, but they are unleashed and released to go and win and make disciples.

OUR TENDER LOVING CARE GROUPS HAVE A TWOFOLD PURPOSE: TO EVANGELIZE AND TO DIS-CIPLE. We see each Tender Loving Care group as being another point of entry into New Hope Community Church. We have not only many need-meeting ministries that become points of entry into New Hope Community church, but every one of our 500-plus Tender Loving Care groups is an outpost into the world and becomes a point of entry through which new converts and members can flow into the body and life of our church.

We not only view every TLC group as a point of entry but we see it also becoming the fence that keeps our members healthy, happy, and in the church. Jesus taught us that there were some similarities between taking care of sheep and taking care of members of the church. Members, like sheep, need the leadership of shepherds. They also need fences to keep them in the flock.

If some of our members begin to stray, they are contacted by their Lay Pastor. If that does not get the job done, then they are approached by their Assistant Pastor. If that does not accomplish getting them back in the fold, then they are visited by their District Pastor. If that doesn't work, then it's brought to my attention as Senior Pastor and I make contact with them. Our plan for keeping people in the fellowship is that they must go past four fences before they can get separated from the fellowship of our church.

Pastor Floyd Schwanz, who supervised our District 4, has this to say about why we need Tender Loving Care groups:

"We have discovered at least four ways our Tender Loving care groups produce growth:

1) The heart-to-heart fellowship experienced in the TLC group is a different dynamic than in our Sunday celebration services. Participants are no longer members of an audience. They are known and know others by name—giving them a feeling that they are an active part of the Body of Christ.

2) Lay Pastors are available for one-to-one care with counsel and prayer about specific needs. Besides being involved directly in evangelism and discipleship, our Lay Pastors also keep in contact with members who become discouraged for a variety of reasons.

3) Individual spiritual gifts are exercised in building up the Body of Christ and reaching the unsaved community.

4) Weekly Bible lessons are written by our Senior Pastor, taught by him to our Lay Pastors, and then used in their

groups. This systematic study of God's Word is not dependent on a few people who can write and present their own lesson plans. Because our Pastor has central leadership in this ministry, tremendous unanimity flows through the life of our congregation.

TEN CHARACTERISTICS OF TENDER LOVING CARE GROUPS

1) **A CLOSE FAMILY**. The more than 5,000 people who attend our Tender Loving Care groups weekly understand this comment that Steven Jones recently made: "My Tender Loving Care group has become closer to me than my own earthly family." As Senior Pastor I have observed that, with four services on Sunday and thousands of people coming and going, the family members from a Tender Loving Care group are on the watch for each other. When they find each other in the crowd it's like a family reunion. There is deep comradeship of belonging one to the other.

There is a deep love that develops one for the other in our Tender Loving Care groups. It is a place where people are known in an impersonal society. It is a place where people are loved in an unloving society. It's a place where people find acceptance and a loving, prayerful response to their personal needs. What a deep heart-to-heart fellowship a Tender Loving Care group becomes!

We observe that in our Tender Loving Care groups synergism takes place—that the "whole is greater than the sum of its parts". The people who attend the home cell group become so much more together than they can ever be isolated and alone.

In our Tender Loving Care groups we know that **"we really do need each other"**.

2) **APPLICATION OF THE BIBLE TO DAILY LIFE.** In a Tender Loving Care group the Bible lesson, which has been taught by either the Senior Pastor or one of the District Pastors in the training session, is given and shared with the people present at the small group fellowship gathering. One of the drawbacks of sermons, no matter how rich they may be, is that they do not lend themselves to feedback and discussion. In the home cell meeting, questions are asked and dialogue and discussion take place. There's not only the

knowledge in the hearing of the Word of God, there is the practical application if it to the daily life. Every lesson is both relevant and applicable.

3) **SHARING OF LIFE'S TESTIMONY.** An important part of Christian life and growth is the sharing of life through testimony. Recounting one's personal victory in Christ builds up the person sharing as well as building up those who hear what God has done. A life lived out is worth many sermons. As people share their life and victories with one another, they also get involved in praying for each other and helping each other. This release of testimony builds great faith and motivates the members of the group to further growth and prayer.

4) **EFFECTIVE ONE-ON-ONE PASTORAL CARE. The TLC group is an effective way to give one-on-one pastoral care to an unlimited number of people.** A steady flow of information flowing down to the Tender Loving Care leaders and flowing back to the pastoral staff enables us to know where and when we need to get involved in back-up ministry.

No church over 100 members can be effective in pastoral care without enlisting and enabling the lay people in the day-to-day pastoral care. In our experience we know that when we have a member who regularly attends a Tender Loving Care group about ninety percent of the pastoral care needed in that person's life is going to be taken care by the leadership of their Tender Loving Care group. Our pastoral staff painfully recognized that the people who never get involved in one of our Tender Loving Care groups are the ones that we have the most difficulty in caring for. **Our highest percentage of membership loss comes from those who never get into one of our TLC groups.**

5) **ENCOURAGEMENT AND EDIFICATION.** Sometime or other everyone of us gets discouraged or down. At the weekly Tender Loving Care meeting, members encourage one another. They also continually edify one another. Where on this earth can people go when they are discouraged? Where can they find personal encouragement? At New Hope Community Church they go to their Tender Loving Care group and this urgent need is met in a beautiful way.

6) **UNLIMITED OPPORTUNITIES FOR MEANINGFUL SERVICE.** One of the things we believe strongly is that everyone

has a desire to serve God in a meaningful way. Our Tender Loving Care groups with their need for leadership provide an unequalled opportunity for lay people to participate in meaningful service. We not only release but train and equip our lay people to do the spiritual work of the ministry in the lives of people. Their work is so important that it makes the difference between hell and heaven, life and death, brokenness and wholeness.

In our Tender Loving Care groups not only does the Lay Pastor who is the leader and the Lay Pastor in training who is the assistant leader have opportunities of meaningful service but each of the persons in the group has the opportunity to minister one to the other. What brings greater joy to life than to minister to another person in Christ's name?

7) **NON-THREATENING FRIENDSHIP EVANGELISM.** Our people are continually encouraged to bring their friends and neighbors and prospects who are funneled to them by means of our communication cards. **Many people who will not attend a church because it is too threatening, will come to a home meeting.** There they are made to feel welcome and comfortable. Non-Christians brought to Tender Loving Care groups, accepted and included and loved, will soon see the love of Jesus in these other people and become hungry and thirsty to know Christ. And when they are brought to Christ through the home cell group, they are already tied into the group for discipling and care in their new-found faith.

8) **DISCIPLING OF NEW CONVERTS.** At New Hope Community Church for the past three years we've been growing at a rate of more than 500 new members a year. More than 80% of these new members are unchurched. Consistently in our Pastor's Classes, which are our membership classes, about 60% of the class members stand and receive the Lord Jesus Christ into their lives as personal Savior. There is no way that we can disciple all these new converts without the Tender Loving Care groups. We know that once we have new converts established in a Tender Loving Care group, they are going to be nurtured in their Christian walk and led into becoming steadfast followers of Jesus. The very best plan in this whole world for discipling is Tender Loving Care groups.

9) **SPIRITUAL GROWTH.** Does the home cell group meeting take the place of church attendance? No. Everyone needs to

hear the preaching of the Word, to be a part of Sunday celebration. However, people who attend our Tender Loving Care groups also get four or five times more benefit out of the Sunday services. How can this be? It's because they are more spiritually alive and in tune with what's happening at the Sunday celebration.

We also have discovered that people's spiritual growth is accelerated many times when they become a part of a dynamic home cell group. There's something about the positive, loving atmosphere of a home cell group that promotes rapid growth in the Christian life. At home cell groups people are given the opportunity to use a variety of spiritual gifts in ministering to one another. As people use their gifts and minister to the edifying of one another, they experience tremendous satisfaction and fulfillment.

10) **DEVELOPMENT OF STRONG LEADERSHIP.** You cannot develop strong leaders by having them sit on the sidelines and watch the pastor do everything. There's an old saying, "Use them or lose them." **As lay people are used in leading Tender Loving Care groups, they develop their leadership skills.** Taking responsibility they become responsible. And as they are faithful in ministry, their ministry keeps enlarging. As they enjoy successes in leadership, they are prepared for bigger assignments. One of the great things that is happening at New Hope Community Church is that we are in the process of developing hundreds of strong leaders. Can you imagine what that's going to mean to our ministry in the years to come? Already I have an exceptional pastoral staff. These excellent workers have come out of our Lay Pastor, home cell organization. **For us, the best is yet to come because we are developing strong leadership.**

PART III - PLAN

CHAPTER 4
THE ORGANIZATIONAL STRUCTURE OF THE TENDER LOVING CARE GROUP AND HOW TO GET A NEW GROUP STARTED

There are three leadership positions in each of our Tender Loving Care groups. 1.) The Tender Loving Care group leader, must be a Lay Pastor. 2.) The Tender Loving Care group assistant leader, who must be a Lay Pastor or a Lay Pastor trainee. 3.) The Tender Loving Care host or hostess.

TENDER LOVING CARE GROUP
LEADER JOB DESCRIPTION
(who must be a Lay Pastor)

1. Make a home visit and phone call for all prospects, members and friendship card assignments.
2. Make sure that 5-6 member families which have been assigned are visited and cared for.
3. Work with the host/hostess to make people comfortable.
4. Talk and pray with the assistant leader and host/ hostess before each week's meeting.
5. Report to the District Pastor each month on the progress of the assistant leader.
6. Initiate the conversational prayer.

7. Lead the Bible lesson and discussion.
8. Be responsible for the report of the TLC meeting.

TENDER LOVING CARE GROUP ASSISTANT LEADER
JOB DESCRIPTION
(who must be a Lay Pastor or a Lay Pastor Trainee)

1. Make a home visit and phone call for all prospects, members and friendship card assignments.
2. Make sure that the 3-4 member families which have been assigned are visited and cared for.
3. Open the meeting.
   (a) Introduce guests
   (b) Icebreaker activity: "Today was a good day because..."

   > "My favorite color is..."
   > "My favorite time of day is..."
   > "One good thing that's happened since last week is..."
4. Make announcements as needed.
5. Lead the sharing time.
6. Plan the refreshment schedule.
7. Arrange for babysitting.
8. Lead the lesson and discussion occasionally on request of the leader.
9. Complete and return the TLC Group Meeting Report sheet.

TENDER LOVING CARE HOST OR HOSTESS
JOB DESCRIPTION

1. Take advantage of the hospitality training which is offered in our church.
2. Provide a comfortable home (or restaurant/business place).
3. Set up refreshments before the meeting time.
4. Arrange chairs in cooperation with the leader.
5. Have extra Bibles and pencils for those who forget theirs.

6. Show people where to put coats.
7. Set an atmosphere of love and acceptance for everyone— regular attenders and guests.
8. Wait until guests have left before cleaning up and rearranging furniture.

WHY IT'S GOOD TO HAVE THESE THREE DIFFERENT LEADERSHIP POSITIONS FILLED

We've had home cell groups where one Lay Pastor or Lay Pastor couple acted as leader, assistant leader, and hosts of the meeting. The problem is that week after week, month after month, this enthusiastic all-out person will burn out. When you have all three leadership positions filled and working, no one gets burned out. If the three get along well and do their jobs, it guarantees a successful Tender Loving Care group. Also, by having an assistant leader, we develop leadership for the starting of another Tender Loving Care group in the coming year.

Many people will open their homes and be marvelous hosts and hostesses but they do not see themselves as potential Lay Pastors and leaders. However, some of these people who start in ministry as hosts or hostesses then see that they, too, can become Lay Pastors leading groups as they naturally aspire and ascend to that place of ministry.

TENDER LOVING CARE MEETING REPORT

Weekly our Lay Pastors fill out a Tender Loving Care Meeting Report and file it at the training meeting they are required to attend. This report is needed to hold the Lay Pastor accountable for what is happening in the Tender Loving Care Meeting. It also provides a continual flow of information so District Pastors can know exactly what is going on.

Every Friday the Senior Pastor receives a detailed report of attendance, number of visitors, converts, contacts made, and how the district is doing on its goals from each of the District Pastors. The District Pastor makes up his report from the sum totals of all the reports that come in from the Tender Loving Care group meetings. On Friday as Senior Pastor I know exactly how many people attended a Tender Loving Care group meeting for the week. I pay close attention to these reports which let me know how we're doing on the reaching of our goals for the year.

HOW TO START A NEW HOME CELL GROUP

The first thing to do when starting a TLC group is to determine who will be the leader, assistant leader and host or hostess.

Next, determine exactly when and where the group will be meeting on a regular weekly basis. Then, set the date for the first meeting. This first meeting should be a time of fellowship and getting acquainted. Serve light refreshments. Your goal is to get people to enjoy being with each other and to challenge them to come back each week for the Tender Loving Care group that is planned.

Where do the people come from? Build your prospect list by writing down anyone and everyone you can think of as a prospective member. In our set up, we have the prospective leader or leaders meet with the District Pastor and work at building the prospect list together. In our church we have thousands of prospects who are divided on our mailing list into the zip codes. Most of those starting a new TLC group can receive almost unlimited prospects from the District Pastor, taken from the mailing list of the poeple who live in that zip code.

However people are not required to attend a Tender Loving Care group in their particular zip code area. The leader may invite anyone whom God has laid on his heart.

Here is the three-part formula that will work every time: build your prospect list—pray your prospect list—and work your prospect list.

WHAT WE ARE LOOKING FOR IN LEADERSHIP
FOR TENDER LOVING CARE GROUPS

1) ENTHUSIASM—Enthusiasm is contagious, and a big part of this is working every day in having a positive attitude. Believe that nothing is impossible with God.

2) CLEAR TESTIMONY—Be able to give a clear direct witness to what Christ has done within your life.

3) DEDICATION—Dedicate yourself to living by the Bible, and being led by the Spirit and dedicated to the Great Mission of New Hope Community Church. Dedicate yourself to building the TLC groups.

4) SPIRIT-LED LIFE—Be filled with the Holy Spirit and daily fellowship with the Holy Spirit. Effective workers are those who are sensitive to the leadership of the Holy Spirit.

5) TIME AND MEANS—Group leaders should not be ones who are all bogged down in their own problems. Be free from bondage in order to serve wholly and effectively.

A SUGGESTED ORDER OF SERVICE FOR A TENDER LOVING CARE GROUP MEETING

	Suggested Time
1. Opening! Introduction of Guests Icebreaker Activity	2
2. Opening Prayer	2

3. Praise: Testimonies
    Singing
    Reports of answered prayer
    Appreciation for each other
    Thanksgiving to God
	10

4. Conversational Prayer	5-10
5. Bible lesson with practical application	30
6. Intercessory prayer to make application of the lesson	5-10
7. Closing Prayer: The Lord's Prayer Doxology	2
	———
	60 minutes

PART III - PLAN

CHAPTER 5 - WHAT TO LOOK FOR IN SUPERVISION

On the job supervision will multiply the effectiveness of your home cell groups many times. It takes leaders to build leaders. If you are a one pastor church, there is no better way to spend your time in ministry than out on the job helping to make the home cell leader successful. Every time you develop a successful leader, you multiply your ministry. In our organization our District Pastors, are responsible for the on-the-job supervision of our Tender Loving Care groups. Here are the seven things that we look for when visiting and supervising one of our Tender Loving Care groups.

1. Check the organization of the leaders (leader, assistant leader, host/hostess).
2. Check the Prospect List (see that it's up-to-date).
3. Check the member families which have been assigned to see that they are being visited.
4. Check progress on the TLC goal (one family added per six months).
5. Name the targeted families.
6. Name any potential Lay Pastors.
7. Observe the use of the 21 Principles for Successful TLC's.
8. Give counsel for how to deal with any "grace-builders"—people who cause difficulty—in the group.

- Items 1 through 5 could be done on the phone when the appointment is made with the leader.
- A report to their superior of the strengths you observed and suggestions for improvement should be made as soon as possible.

PART III - PLAN

CHAPTER 6 - QUESTIONS AND ANSWERS ABOUT LAY PASTORS AND THE CELL SYSTEM

1. IF YOU'RE WANTING TO GET STARTED, WHERE DO YOU BEGIN?

You may not like my answer. **The worst mistake a pastor can make is to divide the whole parish into parts and then assign a leader over each part thinking that suddenly he is going to have all these alive, successful home cell groups.**

The reason this will not work is that people who have not been called and motivated by the Holy Spirit will never follow through on doing the work of ministry. The way to begin home cell ministry is to form one, two, or three groups to begin. The pastor himself should be a part of one of these groups. If other staff pastors are going to work in this important ministry, they also should be a part of one of these first groups. This way the leadership learns the principles firsthand before trying to teach them to others. It takes patient work over three or four years to put the groundwork in before you are ready for mass duplication.

The concept is that first you build leaders. The leaders build groups. Out of these groups come more leaders and a multiplication into more groups.

2. WHERE CAN YOU GO TO GET SOMEONE WHO WILL HEAD UP THIS KIND OF PROGRAM IN YOUR CHURCH?

One mistake I made about three years ago was looking for someone from the outside to head up this ministry in our church, much like one might look for a music man or a youth pastor. This is the wrong approach. For the cell system to be successful it can never be delegated to someone else as a separate ministry. **It must come out of the vision and heart of the Senior Pastor who is in charge.** It must never be another ministry but must be central for the entire body. It is not to be like a music ministry, youth ministry or some other ministry that you hire an associate to do. If it is to be successful, it must be the vision, desire and passion of the leader of the church.

3. DON'T YOU THINK IT'S A LITTLE DANGEROUS TO HAVE ALL THESE LAY PEOPLE RUNNING AROUND DOING THEIR THING?

My answer is, dangerous for what and for whom? Whose church is it anyway? Who's in charge? Who's the administrator, you or the Holy Spirit? One of the things I believe strongly is that the Holy Spirit will, if given time, cleanse His church. **What we need to do is really trust the Holy Spirit with our ministry.**

Over the years I've had a few people get off base someway. Doctrinally off base once in a while, but most of the time critical of my leadership or other things in the church body. The rule is that an unhealthy group will always sooner or later die and the Holy Spirit will cleanse His church. My testimony is that compared to the healthy, successful groups, the unhealthy ones have been a very small number. Certainly not enough to threaten me so that out of my own insecurity I would stop this mighty work of God in our midst.

4. WHAT ABOUT WOMEN IN THE MINISTRY?

One of the greatest resources for the work of ministry in a church today is women. We have multitudes of women who have time to give and who want to make their lives count for the Lord. We believe scripturally that a woman can do anything that a man will give her the authority to do. At New Hope Community Church

I give women the authority to be Lay Pastors and carry on the work of ministry. It is important, if they are married, that they have the approval and blessing of their husbands. We have a number of couples who are Lay Pastors together and work and build their Tender Loving Care group.

5. HOW LARGE SHOULD A HOME CELL GROUP BECOME BEFORE IT'S DIVIDED?

To me, divide is not a good word. **I like the word multiply.** We have Tender Loving Care groups with three or four people. We have many with 8 or 10. We have others that run 20 or 25. My answer is that it depends on the ability of the leader. Participation is the key to success. It takes much more skill as a leader to have 20 people participating in a home cell meeting than it does to get four or five to participate. **Some leaders can handle many people and do an excellent job while others do better with a small number.**

Our whole cell system is built on leadership. We do not begin a new group until we have a leader. Everytime we get a dedicated leader who will commit to our training and live under our leadership, we have the makings of a new, exciting Tender Loving Care group. Continually we encourage our present leaders to keep looking in their groups for new leaders to bring to the Super Bowl training.

6. WHAT IF YOU PASTOR A CHURCH THAT HAS A TRADITIONAL MIDWEEK PRAYER MEETING?

Do not take anything away from the people; give them more. We live in a society of choices. It used to be that when you went to buy a car you had one model to choose from and the color would be black. Today if you go to buy an automobile there are hundreds of choices.

Make your weekly prayer meeting one of the Tender Loving Care groups. Encourage the people who have the habit of going there and who are conditionally tied to that hour and place to keep going. Don't remove their comfort zone. But free the other people to choose other places and times for their home cell meeting. This is the way to break out of the locked-in limitation of one central prayer meeting. You can have many effective home cell groups meeting at different times and places throughout your city.

7. WHERE DO YOU GET THE CURRICULUM?

In every Christian book store you will find numerous sources of small-group Bible study lessons. There is literally a wealth of material available.

For years in our home cell system, we let people choose their own lesson. However, today we write one uniform lesson a week and require that everybody use that lesson. We allow them to adapt that lesson to their particular group needs but believe there is great advantage in having the entire church study the same lesson.

As Senior Pastor I've found it a great advantage in being able to write many of the lessons myself. This enables me to tie the weekly Tender Loving Care lessons into any particular emphasis that I feel the church needs at the time. Often I will tie the lessons into a series that I'm preaching on Sunday mornings.

Throughout the year we vary the lessons. Sometimes they're topical lessons using Scriptures from different parts of the Bible. At other times they are a series like the one we did recently for nine weeks on the Holy Spirit or the one we did for six weeks on how to pray. Right now as I write this, we are in the middle of doing eleven lessons, verse by verse, chapter by chapter from I John. In preparing lessons, remember that "variety is the spice of life." In all of our lessons we write questions that draw the people into dialogue and get them to share and participate, remembering always that the goal is to get people to see the truth of God, understand it and make application in their lives.

A CLOSING WORD

Take whatever you can glean from these pages and from my life of ministry and apply the principles that are universal in your own life and ministry. Please feel free to copy anything that you want to copy. Adapt it and use it any way you can in your local setting.

Be the best you can be. Create the greatest local church that, with God's help, you can create. But remember, you are unique and every church is unique so be yourself. But determine here and now to be better than you were before we journeyed together through the pages of this book. And if that happens, I will be more than repaid for the time spent of sharing my life and ministry with you in these pages.

OTHER MATERIALS AVAILABLE TO HELP YOU IN
LAY PASTOR AND SMALL GROUP MINISTRY

LAY PASTOR TRAINING MANUAL   **COST**

It's a 64-page book with job descriptions, qualifications and standards, report sheets procedures, principles by which we operate, and the nuts and bolts of our home cell group ministry (10% discount when ordering 10 or more).

                                                        $10.00

20/20 VISION IMPACT VIDEO TAPE

(VHS)A one hour instructional video on how to create a successful church with Lay Pastors and cell groups by Dale E. Galloway.

                                                    $19.95

TENDER LOVING CARE GROUP LESSONS FOR ONE YEAR

Three volumes, each volume containing 52 lessons used effectively in our small groups (10% discount when ordering 10 or more).

                                 Volume One $15.00
                                 Volume Two........ $15.00
                                 Volume Three $15.00

THE DEVELOPING DYNAMIC LEADERSHIP SEMINAR MANUAL AND LEADERSHIP TRAINING SEMINAR TAPES

A comprehensive seminar helping you to train effective leaders by Dale E. Galloway.

                                 Manual $15.00
                                 Cassette Tapes $15.00

52 MINISTRY SKILLS FOR SMALL GROUP LEADERS

A tool designed for churches who desire practical lessons to train their Lay Pastors. There are eight subjects on topics such as counseling, leadership skills, theology, and much more. Included with each lesson are cassette tapes narrated by our four district pastors.

                                                    $69.95

ADDITIONAL COPIES OF "20/20 VISION

Available at a cost per copy. (10% discount ordering 10 or more).

                                                    $11.95

Address correspondence to:
Scott Publishing Company
11731 S. E. Stevens Road
Portland, OR. 97266
Phone: (503) 774-8851 or 659-5683

CHURCH GROWTH INSTITUTE
FOUR ACTION-PACKED DAYS
HELD THREE TIMES EACH YEAR
ON THE FIRST WEEKEND OF
FEBRUARY
MAY
OCTOBER

Come to New Hope Community Church and discover how the vision of Acts 20:20 can be successfully put into operation in your local church. Pastor Galloway, members of the staff team and all Lay Pastors will do everything they can to share and help you to be successful in your ministry.

In America today there are some churches that have a little addition every year...there are a few churches that have multiplication...but there is only a handful that have exponential growth. If this kind of growth plus making your life really count effectively for God is important to you, then seeing and experiencing what's happening at New Hope Community Church first hand is a must in your life.